Walking the Way of Jesus

Walking the Way of Jesus

An essay on Christian spirituality

EJ Cuskelly MSC

ST PAULS

ACKNOWLEDGMENTS
Extracts from the *Letterbook* and the *Postio Super Causae Introductione* of Mary MacKillop are used with permission of the Trustees of the Sisters of St Joseph. Extracts from *Journeying With the Lord: Reflections for every day* by Carlo Maria Martini are used with permission of Alba House, New York. Extracts from *No Cowards in the Kingdom* by E J Cuskelly MSC, are used with permission of Spectrum Publications, Richmond. Extracts from *Rule for a New Brother* by H van der Looy, published and © 1973 by Darton, Longman and Todd, are used with permission of the publishers. Extracts from the English translation of the *Catechism of the Catholic Church* for Australia © 1994 St Pauls, Strathfield/Libreria Editrice Vaticana, are used with permission.

Photo insert credits: M Humphries (pages 2,3), M P Stephenson (page 4).

Every effort has been made to acknowledge, in endnotes, the sources of brief texts quoted in this book. Unfortunately, due to the ill health and consequent death of the author, the publishers were not able to obtain from him complete references to all quoted texts. We apologise for any failures to acknowledge sources. We hope to remedy these omissions in any future edition, as information comes to our notice.

WALKING THE WAY OF JESUS: An essay on Christian spirituality

First published May, 1999

National Library of Australia
Cataloguing-in-publication Data:
Cuskelly, Eugene James
Walking the Way of Jesus: An essay on Christian spirituality
ISBN 1 876295 17 1
1. Spirituality. 2. Christian life. I. Title
248.4

Published by
ST PAULS PUBLICATIONS - Society of St Paul
60-70 Broughton Rd - P O Box 906
Strathfield NSW 2135

Cover design by Isabel de Sequera

Printed by Ligare Pty Ltd

ST PAULS PUBLICATIONS is an activity of the priests and brothers of the Society of St Paul who place at the centre of their lives the mission of evangelisation through the means of social communication.

Foreword

Bishop Cuskelly asked to see me shortly before I left for the Synod of Oceania in November 1998. A month earlier he had been diagnosed with a life threatening illness, the treatment of which, although uncomfortable, had prolonged his life. He told me in his direct but always casual manner that in the time remaining he would like to write a small book on spirituality. I was delighted by his suggestion and promised to give him every help possible.

Walking the Way of Jesus is the result. Written in the midst of his illness, it is the spiritual distillation of his life, lived largely in leadership roles in the Church, with the excitement, exhilaration, pain and discomfort of the immediate post Vatican II years. Only one who has exercised leadership in those difficult years can understand its challenges. Bishop James never found leadership easy. His gentle, sensitive nature made its demands somewhat burdensome. Nevertheless, despite that pressure, he led the worldwide Missionaries of the Sacred Heart and the Pastoral Planning of this Archdiocese with vision, courage and compassion.

It is said that one discovers the quality of a person when he or she faces the ultimate trial of death. If this is true, and I believe it is, then no one has edified me more than Bishop James. He approached this time with the deepest faith and courage, as well as a profound desire to use these last precious moments for the benefit of other people. My admiration for him has increased as his life has waned. I have come to better understand the remarkable treasure that he has been to the universal

Church and to the Archdiocese of Brisbane. At this time my heart goes out in a special way to his family and friends, who knew him better than I did, and especially to the members of the Missionary Order of the Sacred Heart of Jesus whom he loved so dearly and led with such distinction.

For those who knew him well and understood the quality of his faith, this book will contain no surprises. For those who did not, the book will introduce them to his faith, his wisdom, his deep peace and his gentle humour. All of us will certainly be better people for having read it.

I am sure that you will join your prayers to mine that the merciful heart of Jesus will comfort him as the shadows fall on his life. Let us pray that Mary, the Mother of Jesus, to whom he had such a deep devotion in these final weeks of his life, and Blessed Mary MacKillop, whom he admired so deeply, will intercede for him and lead him home towards that blessed company of angels and saints where he will live forever.

Sincerely in Christ,

+ John Bathersby
Archbishop of Brisbane

February, 1999

Contents

Preface

In retirement and ill health, I read again these words of the Bengali poet Rabindranath Tagore who said to his God:

> The river has its everyday work to do
> and hastens through fields and hamlets;
> yet its incessant stream winds
> towards the washing of Thy feet.
> The flower fills the air with its sweetness,
> but its last service is to offer itself to Thee.

It seemed that the time for my last service had come. But when my health improved for a while I thought that there was yet time for one more service to the Church of Brisbane in which I had happily spent the first seventeen years and these last seventeen years of my life - and perhaps to other local Churches as well.

When Archbishop Bathersby was appointed to the Archdiocese of Brisbane, he declared that the priorities he wanted for the Church here were *spirituality, justice* and *ecumenism*. Since the word 'spirituality' can be understood in a number of different ways, and since I had written books on the spiritual life, I thought it might be helpful if I were to write a small book setting forth some of the essentials of Christian spirituality. Naturally, I checked with the Archbishop that my exposition was in harmony with his vision. And when I read the theme of the Synod for Oceania, I realised that living a spiritual life could be described as following Jesus, *walking his way, telling his truth, living his life.*

I thank all those who helped me with this book. Given time, with further consultation, it could have been improved. But further time was not given.

Introduction

Train yourself spiritually. Physical exercises are useful enough, but the usefulness of spirituality is unlimited (1 Tim 4: 7-8 *Jerusalem Bible*).

The word 'spirituality' is used with a number of meanings. Even in a stricter sense of a Christian spirituality, it embraces a wide sweep of reality. The *Dictionnaire de Spiritualité* has almost as many volumes as the *British Encyclopedia*. Someone once wrote that there are as many spiritualities as there are men and women, for spirituality is a way of standing before God with one's particular temperament and one's personal gifts.

Hence this small volume has a very modest aim – that of proposing thoughts which may help some people as they try to respond to Jesus' call to 'come follow me'. For, when I write of spirituality I understand a Christian vision of faith which then issues in a response. Even allowing for personal differences, there are some elements that are essentials in any Christian spirituality.

'A vision that issues in a response.' The vision determines the response. Puritans had a vision and a spirituality, so did Jansenists and others who developed a grim outlook on the practice of religion. Therefore it is most important that the vision be healthy and accurate.

By a Christian spirituality I understand *the sum total of those attitudes and actions of a person who believes in the Trinity as the loving source of our being who created us for eternal happiness and who calls us, in this life, to believe in Jesus Christ, to follow his teachings, to cherish his gifts, to love the Lord our God and our neighbour with the self-same love, and to work for the kingdom.*

In planning this work I was helped by a group of friends from the Brisbane Church who generously shared some of their spiritual insights with me. They made a number of points, which to a large extent have determined the contents of this book. For them, some of the key points in the spiritual life of a Christian are the following:

1. We must realise that God is with us in everything we do – in the family and workplace.
2. We need a strong awareness of the presence of God – in people and in creation.
3. We are sent to promote the reign (or kingdom) of God in our world.
4. We live our spiritual life as disciples of Jesus - in the community of the Church.
5. Personal prayer is an important element in the spiritual life.
6. Behind and beneath all other things,
   a) we have to know that God loves us; and
   b) we must strive to radiate that love to others.

We will take up the point of knowing God's love in chapter two of this book. With regard to radiating God's love to others, one of our group recalled a prayer from Cardinal Newman which had been a source of inspiration in her youth and guided her spiritual life through the years :

Lord Jesus fill me with your Spirit.
Let me carry your presence wherever I go.
Look through my eyes, listen through my ears, speak through my lips.
Walk with my feet, love with my heart.
Penetrate me and possess me so fully
that my whole life may be only a reflection of yours.
Shine through me and be in me so completely
that every person I come in contact with
may feel your presence in my soul.
Let me look up and see no longer me but only you.
May my poor presence be a reminder, however weak,
of your divine presence.
Let me preach you not just by words but by my example -
by the catching force, the sympathetic influence of what I do.

1

From practising the faith
to living a spirituality

Once we talked a lot about those members of the Church who *practised*, who *carried out their religious duties*. It was clear what those duties were – going to Mass on Sundays, contributing to the support of our pastors, going to Confession at least once a year, and so on. Certain moral duties were expected of us, most of them indicated by the prescriptions of the Ten Commandments.

Within the Catholic Church the level of *practice* was fairly high, for those were the days when most of us had a strong sense of duty and a respect for authority and for what Church authorities asked of us. Those days are gone and now the Church can no longer consist of people who do their duty and carry out their religious practices. It will be made up of people who, in response to a clear vision of faith, gladly live their Christian life. Religion, for them does not consist in a number of practices to be performed. In the true sense of the word,'religion' binds them to God in a personal relationship, so that the whole of their lives is their response to the revelation they have received. They live a Christian spirituality. Nothing else will do for the Church of the future.

For the majority of practising Catholics in the past, *practising the faith* did grow into a spirituality. For some it did not; and when a crisis of faith occurred, they gave up the practice of the faith. Many Catholics, desiring a deeper spiritual life, joined one of the movements within the Church like the movement for Young Christian Workers, the Charismatic movement and so on. Some associated themselves with Religious Orders and their spirituality. Before the Second Vatican Council, very many of those who wished to live a more intensely spiritual life either entered Religious Life or became priests. In our days the desire for a strong spiritual life does not automatically suggest a vocation to priesthood or cloister.

As we plan for the Church of tomorrow, we need to examine all of our pastoral activities in the light of the changed mentality. A number of our parishes have introduced new practices to answer the new demands. Our Catholic schools, particularly our secondary schools, have faced numerous challenges over the years and are doing their best to answer them. It is no secret that hundreds, even thousands, of young people who go through our schools do not *practise the faith* after they leave. How effectively can the schools set them on the way towards living a Christian spirituality? Are they able to do so? Do the teachers (who are the Church for many of these young people) live their own Christian spirituality? How many school-leavers have said to a living God (though still with the immaturity of youth): 'Yes, I will be a member of your people and you will be my God'? How many of our teachers have made that same commitment?

Our schools would be blessed if our teachers took the recently canonised Edith Stein as their model and patron.

Between 1922 and 1931, the so-called hidden years, she taught German language and literature at St Magdalena's, a girls' academy and teacher-training institute run by Dominican sisters in Speyer. A recent convert, she now understood teaching as a form of apostolate not only pursuing excellence through educative skills, but striving to be personally and religiously influential in the lives of her students, giving good example and generously devoting herself to their needs. 'Surely it is most important that the teachers have the spirit (of Christ) themselves and vividly exemplify it. At the same time they need to know life as the children will find it'.[1]

Living a spirituality, or practising one's religion? Depending on one's attitude there is a vast difference between the way one performs religious duties. For instance, there is a world of difference between those who go to Mass only because it is a duty expected of Catholics and those who go because they have committed their lives to God and are eager to thank God for being gracious to them and to learn what is God's will for them. The first lot find it boring; the second see it as a necessary part of their spiritual life.

In the following pages we shall reflect on what it means to live a Christian spirituality in our contemporary world. It is simple enough to say what are the essentials of a genuine Christian spirituality. They can generally be summed up under the two headings of vision and response.

---

1 Tom Carroll, 'A woman for our times: the gift and promise of St Edith Stein', *Australasian Catholic Record* Vol 75 No 4 (October, 1998), p 462.

2

The vision

'If your eye is healthy, your whole body will be full of light' (Mt 6:22).

A consistent vision of love

Once, in Rome I spent a month working closely with Archbishop (later Cardinal) Joseph Bernardin. On that occasion I learned to appreciate his clarity of thought - a clarity which later shone through his teaching on a 'consistent ethic of life'. With this phrase, he argued strongly and convincingly that our teaching about the dignity of human life should not be a patchwork collection. Identical principles should inspire our teaching about all issues of human life and death: the treatment of the human foetus, abortion, euthanasia and capital punishment. The whole should be 'one seamless garment' (an image taken from Jesus' seamless garment for which the soldiers gambled under the cross). Bernardin's thesis has been widely accepted and used.

I would like to apply the Cardinal's principle to the wider field of our Christian vision of faith. Over many years my own theological teaching and preaching have insisted that central to our faith is 1 John 4:16: what makes us Christians is that we 'have learned to believe in the love that God has for us'. This is a *simple* vision of faith, but it is essential and central. Starting with this truth, ours needs to be a *'consistent* vision of love' – and this is not always the case.

In our days, Christians speak easily of God's love being at the centre of their faith. But – even in our liturgical prayers – we go on to speak in ways that suggest that our vision is not one seamless garment of love. For example, in many a Mass, those who say they believe in God's love go on to say, unthinkingly, 'In justice you condemned us, but in mercy you redeemed us.' Further, when people talk of the passion and death of Jesus, often they speak of God who lays on Jesus' shoulders the punishment for our sin. The prophet Isaiah provided texts that favour this notion: 'For my people's guilt have I smitten him...God laid on his shoulders our guilt, the guilt of us all...' (Isa 53).

Often, different ideas that are not really consistent with one another are bundled together in a way that is simply not logical – and not possible. A consistent vision of love begins with the text from St John: 'God loved the world so much that he sent his only Son' (Jn 3:16). Then it sees *everything* that God does in and through Jesus as totally motivated by love. This is the kind of vision contained in one of our Eucharistic Prayers:

> You sent Jesus your Son among us as Redeemer and Lord.
> He was moved with compassion for the poor and the powerless,
> for the sick and the sinner.
> He made himself neighbour to the oppressed.

By his words and actions he proclaimed to the world,
that you care for us as a father cares for his children.[1]

In justice God redeemed us

As we develop our vision, or explain our theology, we must never 'take away the number we first thought of'. That is, nothing that is part of our faith has its explanation elsewhere than in the love of God. All attempts to explain Christ's redeeming work must keep this in mind.

This redeeming work was announced in the angel's words to St Joseph: 'She (Mary) will give birth to a son, and you must name him Jesus because he is the one who will save his people from their sins' (Mt 1:21).

Often, in explanations of *how* Jesus saves his people from their sins, the seamless garment of love begins to unravel. Metaphors from other days are introduced such as ransom from the slavery of sin. Often, it was said, the blood of Christ was the price that had to be paid for our redemption. Sin needs to be expiated, since it is an offence against an all-holy God. Putting these images with the statement that God is love results in a picture that does not fit easily together. Even though many of these phrases come from sacred Scripture, they are metaphors. Taken literally they distort the real truth.

To test the consistency of your own vision, consider these two quotations from official prayers of the Church. They are, in fact, extracts from the first two weekday Prefaces from *The Roman Missal*:

> 1. Father, all-powerful and ever-living God,
> we do well always and everywhere to give you thanks
> through Jesus Christ Our Lord.
>
> In him you have renewed all things
> and you have given us all a share in his riches.

Though his nature was divine,
he stripped himself of glory
and by shedding his blood on the cross
he brought peace to the world.

Therefore he was exalted above all creatures...

2. ... we do well always and everywhere to give you thanks.

In love you created us,
in justice you condemned us
but in mercy you redeemed us.

The second prayer does what so many of us tend to do. It reads back into Scripture – and into God – a limited notion of human justice – as if, like a human judge, God is obliged to punish and to condemn if a crime has been committed. But, in the Bible, God's justice is his justifying power that he uses to make us just. In justice he *redeems* us – a concept expressed in these words of one of our hymns: 'Free us from sin by might of thy great loving.'[2] The authors of this prayer could well consider a text from the prophet Hosea 11: 8-9 where, speaking of the possibility of punishing Israel, God says: 'My heart recoils within me, my compassion grows warm and tender. I will not execute my fierce anger, I will not destroy Ephraim for I am God and no mortal.' God is able to forgive, being free from the human need to punish.

The first weekday Preface I quoted will sound familiar to most, for they will see it as a paraphrase of St Paul's letter to the Philippians (2:6-7). St Jerome's Latin translation of Philippians 2:6 reads: '*Deus cum esset*'. The Latin word *cum* can mean 'since' or 'although'. The translators of our English prayer have chosen to translate it 'though his nature was divine'. This could suggest that, almost grudgingly, God took on our human nature. However, it would be far more consistent with our image of a loving God to translate the passage, or to paraphrase it: 'Since he was God – the wonderfully compassionate God revealed by Jesus Christ, eager to show how much he cared for us, he gladly emptied himself and suffered and died.' It is not easy for us to grasp the idea of an infinitely loving God, or to cling to the conviction that 'God *is* compassion and love' (Ps 102), but we need to do so.

In the course of history, a number of different metaphors have been used to give some idea of how Jesus saved us from our sin: metaphors of ransom from slavery, of the lamb that was slain, of Old Testament sacrifices and so on. But I believe that it would be more helpful for us to start elsewhere. What is the sin from which men and women needed to be redeemed?

Psalm 106:7 says: 'Our sin is the sin of our ancestors; we have done wrong, our deeds have been evil. Our ancestors when they were in Egypt paid no heed to your wonderful deeds. *They forgot the greatness of your love.*'

The sin that separates us from God is the failure to believe in the wonderful, transforming love of God. Though reasons for this failure are many, the sin is always the same. Now how do we pass from sin to grace, from death to life? St John, in the text already quoted, gives the answer: 'We ourselves have known and put our faith in God's love towards ourselves. God is love and those who live in love live in God and God lives in them' (1 Jn 4:16).

We pass from sin to life by believing in God's love for us and for all people and for the world that God made – and then letting that love rule our lives.

Therefore, when we say that Jesus came to redeem us, to save us from sin, we can express this in another way by saying that Jesus came to enable us to believe in his love for us – to believe that, in all things, God is a loving God. The great theologian, St Thomas Aquinas, wrote that 'there was no more fitting way to free the human race than through the passion of Christ...that men and women might come to know how much God loves them, and that thus they might be brought to love God, for it is in the love of God that the perfection of human salvation consists. This is why the Apostle has said: 'What proves that God loves us is that Christ died for us while we were still sinners''' (Rom 5:8-9).[3]

William of St Thierry wrote: 'Now how is it that we are saved by you, O Lord...if it is not in receiving from you the gift of loving you and being loved by you.'[4]

If we are brought to recognise the love that God has for us and for every human being, then our lives are transformed. St Paul's description of love is the description of a world redeemed: 'Love is always patient and kind; it is never jealous; love is never boastful or conceited, it is never rude or selfish; it does not take offence and is never resentful. Love takes no pleasure in other people's sins but delights in the truth. It is always ready to excuse, to trust, to hope and to endure whatever comes' (1 Cor 13: 4-7).

One reason why some find it difficult to believe in a loving God is what is called 'the problem of evil'. Wrestling with this problem, a New York rabbi once wrote a book called *When Bad Things Happen to Good People*.[5] It is a problem we all encounter. For some it destroys faith or makes it impossible to believe in a loving God. If God is a God of love why does God permit so much evil in the world – sickness, starvation, destruction, catastrophes?

I doubt if anyone finds a satisfactory solution to this problem and then decides to believe. The answer does not come through our reason. First comes faith, which is God's gift. We believe that God is a God of love. Then we can look for an intellectual explanation of why a loving God permits suffering. If this explanation is to be a part of a consistent vision of love it cannot claim that God punishes people for their sins through these natural causes.

My own explanation is not very deep; but it is consistent with faith in a loving God. It is an explanation I learned from a young couple who came to see me before they married. There was asthma in their families. So they faced this choice: would they marry and have children who would be asthmatics, or would they decide not to have children at all? They reasoned that they had received so much happiness from the loving life in their own families that it was better to share that love with others, even though the children would suffer from asthma.

In a way God had a similar choice. Father, Son and Spirit could share their life with creatures. But all created beings are limited, able to suffer. God's wise judgment was that it was better to share the life and happiness of the Trinity with human beings who, after their own share of human happiness in this life, would pass to the unending joy of life eternal. Being creatures, they were subject to human limitations; some suffering would be part of their lives. But the overall balance would be positive. Whatever be our explanation of why God permits suffering, it cannot call into doubt our belief that in all things God is a loving God.

Loving the world so much God sent the Son so that men and women might believe in a loving God. For one reason or another (problem of evil or other problems) many of them felt that God, if God there was, did not care about them. Jesus' disciples were not the first to cry out: 'Do you not care that we are perishing?' (Mk 4: 39) God's problem, if we might put it that way, was to convince men and women that God is a God who cares.

Will you drink the cup that we must drink?

'Do you not care that we suffer leprosy and cancer; do you not care that we suffer injustice and violence and hunger?' The background to the incarnation was that God heard these cries of the poor. The cries could be phrased as a challenge to God, for often they were so phrased: 'Will you drink the cup that we must drink? The cup of our suffering, our dying, our loneliness and our despair?' When Jesus consented to do this he chose the most effective way of showing us that indeed, God is a God who cares. He emptied himself, taking the form of a slave, dying on a cross. God sent the only Son to drink the cup that we must drink, so that we might learn to believe in God's love.

St Thomas Aquinas suggested something like this. He wrote of the different types of sufferings that Jesus endured. And, in what is a free but accurate paraphrase, he said:

> Jesus drank the full cup of our human suffering - betrayed by Judas, denied by Peter; he drank the cup of being deserted by his friends, of being blasphemed and defamed. He suffered in his honour and esteem through

the mockery and lies directed against him. He suffered in his possessions since even his clothing was taken from him. He suffered in his soul, drinking the cup of sadness, repugnance and fear. He suffered in his body through the wounds and the scourging.[6]

St Thomas goes on to detail the sufferings of Jesus' death and dying which we know from the passion narratives in the gospels. The whole picture is that of Jesus' detailed drinking of the cup that we must drink or, in the words of Hebrews 2:9, 'so that, by the grace of God, he might *taste* death for everyone'.

To quote William of St Thierry again: 'Everything he (Jesus) did and everything he said on earth, even the insults, the spitting, the buffeting, the cross and the grave, all that was nothing but yourself speaking in the Son, appealing to us by your love, and stirring up our love for you.'[7] In Mark's Gospel we see Jesus in Gethsemane drinking the cup of our loneliness and our fear.

The words of the Irish poet, Brendan Kennelly, in *The Man of Rain* come to mind: 'The loneliest cry I ever heard .... *Thy will be done*. How lonely was God to decide to make a man who'd cry like that.'

God is rich in mercy

In 1980 John Paul II felt the need to write an encyclical letter to all the faithful reminding them that God is rich in mercy.[8] It would seem that he had two reasons, principally, for writing this letter. The first was that all of us who are conscious of our sinfulness and our need of forgiveness should never doubt the greatness of God's love. 'Love is more powerful than death; more powerful than sin.'[9] No matter what our sin, no matter how great our need for forgiveness, the merciful love of Christ is always there for those who seek it. The Pope, naturally, refers us to the parables of mercy in the Gospel of Luke.

In his commentary on this Gospel, William Barclay has a most interesting and instructive passage about some of the parables, namely the three which occur in the Gospel reading for the Twenty-fourth Sunday in Ordinary Time of Year C (Lk 15:1-32). The three parables in this passage are, firstly, that of the shepherd who, losing one of his sheep, goes in search of it; secondly, the story of the woman who loses a coin and searches carefully until she finds it; and thirdly the parable of the prodigal son who returns to his father. In the first two stories, shepherd and woman call their neighbours together to rejoice when they find the sheep and the coin they had lost. In the third parable the father organises a feast of rejoicing. According to Barclay, at that time there was a saying among the Pharisees that 'there will be joy in heaven over one sinner who is obliterated'.[10] When Jesus heard this saying he knew that it was not true of the Father whom he knew and loved. So, emphatically and in three different ways, he told stories which concluded 'there will be *rejoicing* in heaven over one sinner who *repents*.' That is the kind of God he knew; that is the God in whom, by faith, we have learned to believe.

The second point that the Pope wished to make in his encyclical is that, in a world that puts much stress on justice, we need to see that efforts to be just are tempered with mercy. In our modern world, many a call for justice is really a call for vengeance, motivated at times by 'spite, hatred and even cruelty'. The Pope says that a concept of justice founded on the text 'an eye for an eye and a tooth for a tooth' (Ex 21:24) was a form of distortion of justice, 'and today's forms continue to be modelled on it.'[11]

The Pope goes on to say: 'justice alone is not enough...it can even lead to the negation and destruction of itself, if *that deeper power, which is love*, is not allowed to shape human life in its various dimensions.'[12] There is not a time for love and then a separate time for justice. Without love there can be no true human justice. The wider import of what the Pope is saying is that – if ever you set love aside from your way of acting, some human distortion will enter in.

Set love aside and you enter into the regions of sin. Earlier, we have seen that sin is either a failure to recognise the love of God, or worse, a deliberate rejection of that love. That rejection, that setting aside of love, is clearly evident in the way in which Jesus was rejected and put to death:

> As far as we know, Jesus went around doing good and was put to death for precisely that. He preached God as totally good, forgiving and *for* human life, and this amounted to a confrontation with the given religious and political culture. It was not only the leaders who rejected him. In a sense one can see a certain inevitability in this, and once one does, once one grasps this inevitability, one is standing nakedly before the radical sinfulness of human nature. The violent execution of Jesus is a revelation of the sinfulness of the human condition, and it appears strikingly in inverse proportion to the sheer goodness and love of God that is disclosed in or through Jesus' love and concern for his fellow human beings. Jesus died because of our sin.[13]

We believe in the love of God present in the world. At the same time we cannot ignore the presence of sin - in the world and in ourselves. Nor can we be surprised by the hatred of human beings and the way that, too often, it is directed against the good, even as it was in Jesus' day.

Our view of the Church, too, must find a place that is consistent with our vision of a loving God revealed in Christ. There can be no place for opinions like that of Leonard Feeney who was condemned for teaching that only members of the Catholic Church could be saved. The Church was founded for salvation not for condemnation. Vatican II spoke of the Church as a *sacrament* of salvation. It is the visible sign of God's love uniting humankind to God – a sign of God's love for the world. In the next chapter, we shall see the consequences of this truth.

1 *Eucharistic Prayer for Masses for Various Needs and Occasions*, International Committee on English in the Liturgy.

2 From 'God of Thy Pity', *Ante-Tridentine Breviary* translated by Alan G McDougall. Search Press.

3 *Summa Theologiae*, III q 46 a 3.

4 *On Contemplating God.*

5 Harold S Kushner, *When Bad Things Happen to Good People*, London: Pan Books, 1981.

6 *Summa Theologiae*, III, q 45, a 5.

7 *On Contemplating God.*

8 John Paul II, Encyclical letter *On the Mercy of God* (*Dives in misericordia*), 1980.

9 *Dives in misericordia*, n 8.

10 William Barclay, *The Gospel of Luke*, rev ed, Edinburgh: The Saint Andrew Press, 1975, p 200.

11 *Dives in misericordia*, n 12.

12 *Ibid.*

13 R Haight, *An Alternative Vision*, New York: Paulist Press, 1985, pp. 128-9.

3

The response

Christian, recognise your dignity

What is, or what should be, our response to the revelation of God's love? In the spiritual life, if our vision of God is right, the response will be healthy. When we accept that a loving God wants us to be God's people and when we say, 'Yes, you will be our God,' then our first response will be to recognise and acknowledge the reality of what has occurred in our lives. In the classic phrase of Leo the Great: *Christian, recognise your dignity and live accordingly.*

Following Jesus' teaching in the gospels, our response will be *to love the Lord our God and our neighbour as ourselves.* How we are to do this in practice in our modern world will be spelt out in the following pages. But firstly let us give some thought to what it means to love our fellow human beings. Towards people we have never met, we cannot feel the kind of love that we feel for family or close friends. That would be too much. On the other hand, it is too little to do no more than say that we wish them well. I have found that a very useful way to reflect on this call to charity is to think of the word *respect*. It comes from the Latin, *respicere*, to look again. The derivation suggests that every human being is worth a second look. If you look quickly, fleetingly, you see a face you may not recognise. But, look again, deliberately, and you see someone with human dignity, called to be a child of God. And if you look with respect, you are on the way to love; without respect there can be no true love.

The Christian response to faith in God's love for the world that God made will extend, too, to all creation – respect for God's gifts, for the environment in which we live.

And how do we 'love the Lord our God'? Pope John Paul II has expressed the reality in this way:

> With Baptism we become *children of God in his only-begotten Son, Jesus Christ.* Rising from the waters of the Baptismal font, every Christian hears again the voice that was once heard on the banks of the Jordan River: 'You are my beloved son/daughter, with you I am well pleased' (Lk 3:22). From this comes the understanding that one has been brought into association with the beloved Son, becoming a child of adoption (cf Gal 4:4-7) and a brother or sister of Christ.[1]

This is why St Paul addresses his converts as 'brothers and sisters whom the Lord loves' (2 Thess 2:13) and exhorts them to 'try then to imitate God as children of his that he loves' (Eph 5:1).

True spirituality begins when God enters your life - and, under the influence of God's grace, is accepted as your God and when you delight in being a son or daughter of God: 'The Holy Spirit is poured forth in our hearts to enable us to cry *Abba, Father'* (cf Rom 5:5).

Then those 'who enter into Thee enter into the joy of their Lord'.[2] We truly enter into the Lord – or let the Lord enter into our lives – if, in the process, joy enters into our hearts. This truth was brought home to me a number of years ago when I met Mary Rose Moore from a small town in Texas, USA. In fact, we 'met' only by letter and telephone. She wrote to me to tell me that, in studying to enter the Catholic Church, she had read a book that I had written and had found it helpful. As she and her six small children prepared for their reception into the Church she felt that she would like to write to me, sending photos of the children, pigtails, tooth-braces and happy smiles. Naturally I was pleased to 'meet' people whom I had helped on their spiritual journey.

Then, not long afterwards, she wrote to tell me two things. Firstly she was delighted that, so soon after her entry into the Catholic Church, she had been approved as a teacher of Catholic doctrine. Secondly, the doctors had discovered that she had a tumour of the brain. They estimated that she had no more than two years to live. Then she asked me to pray for her.

At this point in my reading I put down her letter and speculated as to what she would ask me to pray for – perhaps that she might be cured, perhaps that, after she had gone, her children might be well cared for. But she asked for neither of these things. She had learned to believe in a loving God, Father to her and to her children. Into God's hands she could entrust her soul, as also she could entrust her children's future.

She asked me to pray that 'in the time left to me, as I teach Christian doctrine, I might share with others something of the joy that the faith has brought into my life.' Obviously she had learned the lesson of Psalm 31:7: 'But my trust is in Yahweh; I will delight and rejoice in your faithful love'.

I believe that, at the heart of every genuine vocation to ministry that same desire exists: 'That I might share with others something of the joy that the faith has brought into my life'. The joyless calls are no true calls at all; and often the so-called 'vocation that fails' does so because there was never any joy at its heart.

A pertinent text occurs in 1 Chronicles 29:17. It is part of the prayer of David as he offered to the Lord the precious materials he had gathered for the building of the temple. David prayed: 'In the simplicity of my heart, joyfully have I offered (*laetus obtuli*) all these things...O Lord God of Israel, keep us constant in the gladness of our giving.' For me this text sums up a thesis which contains several elements:

There is no spiritual life without conversion. Conversion I understand not primarily nor necessarily as a turning away from sin, but a turning to – a giving to God, giving the precious thing of one's own life in whatever vocation is mine. The rich young man of the Gospel was a good man, but he could not give gladly to the Lord – 'He went away sad' (Mk 10:22).

At some point in our lives, in some way, every follower of Christ is invited to give his or her life to the Lord. For Augustine, and for others, this turning to the Lord meant also a marked turning away from a sinful life. For many, it is simply a step forward from a fairly ordinary life – or the realisation that, if you walk with God, life ceases to be ordinary. Yet – the nature of such a call (with the realisation of what we could have done and not succeeded in doing) is such that each of us will pray: 'With an honest heart joyfully have I offered all these things' (cf 1 Chron 29:17). This is true of any committed Christian.

And all of us need to pray: *'Domine Deus, conserva hanc voluntatem'*, – 'Lord God, keep us constant in the gladness of our giving'. For, if ever we cease to give gladly and generously, the light has gone from our lives and the heart of our vocation has died.

For all of us, there will be tough times when we will be tempted to regret the act of giving and to take back the gift we once offered. Then it is that we are called to re-affirm the offering we once made and to go on giving.

The whole of our lives is given to God

Our first response is to recognise, delight in, and be grateful for the fact that, by God's grace we have become children of God. A second response is to realise that, therefore, all our human activity has value in God's sight. There is a unity in the Christian vocation. It is not partly secular, partly religious, but rather a dedication of one's whole life to Christ and to the kingdom. The document *Christifideles laici* puts this very well :

> There cannot be two parallel lives in their existence; on the one hand the so-called 'spiritual' life, with its values and demands, and, on the other, the so-called 'secular' life, that is, life in a family, at work, in social relationships, in the responsibilities of public life and in culture. The branch, engrafted into the true vine which is Christ, bears its fruit in every sphere of existence and activity. In fact, every area of the lay faithful's lives, as different as they are, enters into the plan of God, who desires that these very areas be the 'places in time' where the love of Christ

is revealed and realised for both the glory of the Father and service to others.

Every activity, every situation, every precise responsibility – as, for example, skill and solidarity in work, love and dedication in the family and the education of children, service to society and public life and the promotion of truth in the area of culture – are the occasions ordained by Providence for a 'continuous exercise of faith, hope and charity.'[3]

Vatican II had similar teaching, seeing all Christian effort brought together to be offered to God in the Eucharistic celebration:

For their work, prayers and apostolic endeavours, their ordinary married and family life, their daily labour, their mental and physical relaxation, if carried out in the Spirit, and even the hardships of life if patiently borne - all of these become spiritual sacrifices acceptable to God through Jesus Christ (cf 1 Pet 2:5). During the celebration of the Eucharist, these sacrifices are most lovingly offered to the Father, along with the Lord's body. Thus, as worshippers whose every deed is holy, the lay faithful consecrate the world itself to God.[4]

John Kavanaugh has written that:

It is first and foremost in our relationships, our families, our friends, that God is encountered, that faith is given flesh, that our theories of justice are tested, that our prayer is made real, that dreams are actualised...Our most profound sufferings, our greatest heroics, our most significant encounters with God, are here with these people we know and love, in their goodness, in their weakness. Where else do we most intimately encounter what Paul calls the 'requirements of love', those crucibles of patience, the winnowing of humility, the courage of forgiveness, the comfort of kindness.[5]

In the Church

• *The Church of the poor*

At baptism we become members of the Church. Our view of the Church will be influenced by St Peter's words: 'You are a consecrated nation, a people set apart to sing the praises of God who called you out of darkness into his wonderful light' (1 Pet 2:9).

These are beautiful phrases; and of course they are true. But they need to be balanced by another truth. The Church is the Church of the poor, the *anawim*, the little ones who acknowledge their poverty and their need of God's saving grace. I believe that a number of those who have left the Church have done so because they did not believe in the Church of the poor. I do not mean here that the Church needs to have a concern for the poor, the oppressed, the marginalised. That we take for granted. It must be true today, as it always was, that 'the Good News is proclaimed to the poor' (Mt 11:5). But over and above that, we need to accept that we are a Church made up of 'the poor'.

There is a wonderful passage in chapter 9 of the book of Deuteronomy where Moses tells the people of Israel that Yahweh had threatened to destroy them because of their infidelity. God promised to then give to Moses a 'mightier and more numerous nation' (9:14) to lead into the promised land. Moses related how he 'pleaded with Yahweh: "My Lord Yahweh, do not destroy your people, your heritage"' (9:26). Moses carried on with a good piece of oriental bargaining, saying that it would do God's reputation no good to destroy the people whom God had led out of Egypt. But, in reality, Moses knew that a second group would be no more perfect than the first. The

People of God is a group of very human, limited people, all of them needing redemption from selfishness and sin.

This is true of the Church in every age. In Jesus' parable, it is not the perfect but the 'poor, the blind and the lame' who are invited to the feast (Lk 14:21). There are poor and lame in every country. There are blind people on all the ways of the world; there are people with their limited intelligence, their disabilities, their poverty. There are no other kinds of people but these. These are the men and women who make up the People of God. Even those who are asked to lead us, to be our bishops our popes and our priests, are fashioned from the same human stuff as this. And because this is so, there are some who say they can't stand the limitations and the pettiness of it all and justify their leaving the Church.

What sort of a Church did they think they believed in? One of the oldest heresies is that of seeking a Church made up only of the perfect, a heresy that has expressed itself in different forms from the Priscillianists right to our own day. Here one is forced to marvel at human inconsistency. Before Vatican II there were those who rejected the Church because, they said, it was arrogant, claiming to be the one, holy catholic Church. Then, in the Council, it confessed to be a Church of sinners, imperfect and in need of reform. Now there are those who leave it, justifying their actions by statements about the Church's imperfections – as if the Pilgrim People of God could be a perfect people.

The Church is the Church of the poor – but there is a deeper poverty than that of material want – the poverty of darkness and doubt, of limited ideas and simply not knowing what to do to heal the world. If we cannot accept the Church with all its human limitations, then we are not being very realistic. The Word of God became incarnate with all the limitations of our human nature. Christ lives on in the Church with its human limitations, even with its sin from which it looks to him for forgiveness and redemption.

The Church's imperfections are often depressing, sometimes frustrating. They are depressing and hurtful, especially when some of its members are unworthy of their calling. Many people suffer when those who are called to be ministers of pastoral charity betray their trust and abuse the 'little ones' entrusted to their care. The victims suffer most; and all those good people suffer who love the Church and work to make it the sacrament of God's love for the world.

Other imperfections which are not sinful can yet be terribly frustrating for people at every level of the Church. There is no point in enumerating the different ways in which we can feel frustrated in the Church. Our task is to walk the way of Christ through this imperfect world. Giving way to frustration is our failure not the fault of others; we must not let frustration defeat us.

• *The Church – a community of hope*

'Know that I am with you always, yes, to the end of time' (Mt 28:20). So ends Matthew's Gospel – with a phrase which has brought strength and consolation to many generations of God's pilgrim people. Before that, the Hebrew people, too, had found a source of strength in God's promises to be with them.

Every group, every generation and every culture has had its own way of seeing the signs of God's presence. Without always formulating it, each has developed its own theology of the way in which God will be with the people. And, for every generation as for every individual, part of living the paschal mystery is seeing our own hopes die only to discover that God is with us in ways in which we never dreamed. And some of us, like Jesus, must die trusting that God will be with the people, without knowing how this will be.

We read in the Hebrew Scriptures that the People of God trusted in God's promises to be with them always. As everyone tends to do, they then worked out their theological theories of *how* God would be with them. There were at least three elements in their theology of God's presence among them.

First of all, in a conviction that began with the Exodus, they saw Yahweh as the Lord God of armies, *Dominus Deus Sabaoth*, the God who fought with their fighters to bring them victory. In Moses' words: 'The Lord will fight for you' (Ex 14:14). Later, in one of the classic battles of all time, David would say as he went to fight Goliath: 'You come to me with sword and spear and dagger, but I come against you in the name of the Lord God of hosts, the God of the ranks of Israel' (1 Sam 17:45). To this God of armies the great leaders of Israel, like Judas Maccabaeus, prayed as they went into battle, 'All praise to you, Saviour of Israel, who by the hand of your servant David broke the giant's onslaught' (1 Macc 4:30).

A second sign of God's being with the people is seen in the prosperity bestowed on them in their days of peace: 'Then the Lord blessed the end of Job's life more than the beginning: he had fourteen thousand sheep and six thousand camels, a thousand yoke of oxen (sheep and cattle galore) and as many she donkeys. He also had seven sons and three daughters (*perfect numbers*

7 and 3). There were no women in the entire world so beautiful as Job's daughters' (Job 42:12-13, 15). Beautiful daughters, vines heavy with grapes, trees laden with fruit, plentiful harvests, flocks and herds in abundance were a sure sign that God was smiling on them.

Thirdly, from the days of Solomon on, the Temple was the place where God dwelt in a special fashion among God's chosen people. In 1 Kings 9:3 God is portrayed as saying, 'I have consecrated this house which you have built to receive my name for all time and my eyes and my heart will be fixed on it forever.' However, the Hebrews forgot the phrases that followed: 'but if you or your sons turn away from following me and do not observe my commandments...this house will become a ruin' (9:6, 8). They did not heed these words. For them the Temple was indestructible and the sure sign of God with them forever. Jeremiah tried to warn them: 'You keep saying, this place is the temple of the Lord, the temple of the Lord, the temple of the Lord. This slogan of yours is a lie. Put no trust in it. If you amend your ways and your deeds...then I will let you live in this place, in the land which long ago I gave to your ancestors' (Jer 7: 4-7).

So they had three signs of God's being with them – the fertile and fruitful land, the splendid Temple standing proud on Jerusalem's hill, and the Lord God of armies marching with them into battle. Then, suddenly all were gone – the land laid waste, their armies routed, their Temple destroyed. Where now was their God? You can imagine their despair; their utter desolation: 'O, God, why have you forsaken us?' (Ps 22:1). And again the prayer of Azariah in the book of Daniel (3:38): 'We have been brought low this day in all the world because of our sins and at this time there is no prince or prophet or leader, no burnt offering or sacrifice or oblation or incense, no place to make an offering before you or to find mercy.'

Perhaps they needed the Exile to learn 'to amend their ways and their deeds, to deal fairly with one another, to cease to oppress the alien, the fatherless and the widow, to shed no innocent blood or run after other gods to their own ruin' (Jer 7:6). Certainly, they needed to believe and trust in God, and not in any of the signs that, in their thinking, were the ways in which God *had* to be with them.

This is a lesson we all must learn. In our time, we too have established our signs of God's presence. And when they are no longer there, or seem to be fading away, then we are afraid that God may be no longer with us – because God is not with us in our way. Our stalls, too, stand empty – in our seminary chapels, in some of our churches. Is God no longer with us? Or is it that God is not with us in the ways that we expect? What are the ways in which we have become accustomed to seeing, or feeling that God is with the Church? Some of the conservative groups in the Church are afraid to let go of old things (for example, the Latin Mass) through which they feel that God has been with the Church.

As we read the New Testament, we see how the followers of Jesus had to revise their expectations about the work of Jesus and what he would do: 'When will you restore the kingdom to Israel?' (Acts 1:6). That is what they expected – that Jesus would deliver them from their Roman conquerors and restore an independent kingdom of Israel. Then we see two of them on the road to Emmaus (Lk 24:13-35), their hopes dashed, their expectations disappointed: We had hoped – for what? 'That he was the one to redeem Israel' as Moses had redeemed Israel from Egypt. We had hoped, but now we hope no more.

After the resurrection the followers of Jesus did not expect a new Church separate from the religion of Israel. They expected a renewed Israel, worshipping in the temple with all the splendid Jewish liturgies followed by their 'Christian' prayers and celebrations. But then, to their dismay, they were cast out of the synagogue when Rabbi Gamaliel II added an extra blessing (which was really a curse on Christians) to the eighteen blessings of the Jewish morning prayer – the *birkat ha-minim* (the blessing of the heretics). Inserted as the twelfth blessing it was to be prayed aloud, and anyone who refused to pray it was thrown out of the synagogue (in fulfilment of Jesus' prophecy): 'For the apostates may there be no hope and may the Nazarenes (that is, the followers of Jesus of Nazareth) and the heretics suddenly perish'. This happened about 85 CE. You can imagine what a shattering experience it was. The letter to the Hebrews was written to encourage the Hebrew Christians, who found themselves with no temple, no ceremonial, but only meetings in a home (the first home Masses). They had to fashion a different liturgy, worship in a different place.

At least two of the Gospels, each in its different fashion, were written to encourage people who, in one way or another, had not seen their expectations fulfilled.

St John of the Cross was a great master of the spiritual life. One of the principles he laid down for all those trying to live a truly spiritual life is that we all need to pass through a period of purification of hope. We tend to rely on ourselves more than on God, on our own efforts more than on God's grace, we have our own human expectations of the way in which we think God will act. Often we have to let go of our own ideas and accept the ways of God that are not our ways. The more we are involved in 'Church', the more we suffer when we see the Church seeming to fail – at least failing to live up to our expectations. But we are always called to be a Church of hope, trusting that Christ will be with his Church even to the end of the world – and often in ways that we do not expect.

• *The Church and the world*

'You are a chosen race' (1 Pet 2:9). St Peter applies these words from the Old Testament to the Church, the new People of God – you are a chosen race, a royal priesthood.

That phrase can be interpreted in quite different ways. Your interpretation will determine your spirituality. Some have interpreted the phrase to mean 'you are the chosen ones, while others are passed over or rejected.' Or it can mean 'you are a chosen group, chosen for the purpose of providing a special service to others who do not join your group.'

The first interpretation influenced the thinking of a number of Catholics before the Second Vatican Council. Certain images such as the Church being the 'ark of salvation'(1 Pet 3:20) or the 'barque of Peter' re-enforced this thinking. Certainly, those who did not get aboard Noah's ark were in big trouble. Applying this image to the Church, sometime in the 1940's, Fr Leonard Feeney, of Boston, USA, taught that all those who were outside the Catholic Church would be damned. Rome condemned this teaching; but the mere fact that it could be formulated and accepted by some showed the way many Catholics were thinking. Most of us had been taught the traditional phrase that 'outside the Church there is no salvation'. Attempted explanations did little to satisfy us.

As we looked around and studied statistics, we were uneasy with having so many people 'outside the Church'. Some of us offered our own theological theories about how they could be saved. Still there was a strong conviction that the task of the Church was to convert as many people as possible – not just from paganism but also from 'heresy' – for their own salvation. For example, in Holland, before the Second Vatican Council, the *Una Sancta* movement was totally aimed at converting non-Catholics, so that there would be 'one holy' Catholic Church.

Then Vatican II set us free – it formulated a teaching on the Church that, at last, was consistent with our vision of a loving God at work in the world. In what was considered one of the most significant statements of the Council, it asserted that the Church is the 'universal sacrament of salvation',[6] 'a kind of sacrament or sign of intimate unity with God and of the unity of all mankind'.[7]

A sacrament exists for the salvation of those whom it affects. As I wrote in an earlier work:

> The Church is in the world and for the world's salvation –
> not in the sense that all people will belong to her (and
> that we fail if we fail to convert others) – but because

she is to be a sign, and somehow a cause of, salvation for all those who consent to be saved by God.[8]

Karl Rahner has written:

The Church is not simply the sign of God's mercy for those who explicitly belong to it. It is the mighty proclamation of grace that has already been given for the world, and of the victory of this grace in the world.[9]

Inspired by this teaching, we wrote things like this:

The Church's main concern... must be... that she should be truly the sacrament of salvation to the world. This will have two areas:
a. Her inner life: As 'sacrament' the Church must be concerned that the divine life is really alive and at work within her, in her faith, her liturgy, her sanctity, her charity.
b. She is sacrament and sign to the world....For this reason she must examine carefully all the ways in which she speaks to the men and women of her time. By what she is and does and says, she must 'preach to the whole world' the Gospel of God's love and mercy. This is a love which is fulfilling, but it is a love which challenges the world.[10]

We were delighted that what we had long suspected was now stated officially – the God of love was at work in the world saving those who were unable to embrace the Catholic faith, namely, all those who 'sincerely seek God, and moved by his grace, strive by their deeds to do his will, as it is known to them through the dictates of their conscience.'[11]

In the teaching of the Council we found a doctrine which was consistent with the vision of a God who was truly a God of love:

Whether it aids the world, or whether it benefits from it, the Church has one sole purpose – that the kingdom of God may come and the salvation of the human race may be accomplished. Every benefit the people of God can confer on mankind during its earthly pilgrimage is rooted in 'the Church being the universal sacrament of salvation' at once manifesting and actualising the mystery of God's love for mankind.[12]

That is, the Church must show, and preach and witness to God's love for all humankind, and it must, in fact, be a group of people who do really show their love for all their brothers and sisters.

Further, Vatican II launched the whole Church on the road of ecumenical activity. Thus we were able to discover, in friendship, the riches of other Christian traditions. Many years later, it was stated that this effort, too, was a consequence of the discovery of that truth that the Church is 'the sacrament of salvation'. The latest Vatican document on ecumenism states: 'Their ecumenical activity will be inspired and guided by a true understanding of the Church as "a sacrament or instrumental sign of intimate union with God, and of unity of the whole human race".'[13]

One debate among missionaries was solved: Should we work for the evangelisation of peoples or for their human development? The solution was simple: we were to work for the 'humanisation' of peoples, that is, for their total human and spiritual growth. This included preaching the gospel and digging wells for clean water when water was needed.

Obviously the Vatican Council gave us a more open, more charitable (and therefore more Christian) attitude towards our fellow human beings. 'Heretics' became our Christian brothers and sisters; 'infidels' were seen as 'men and women of good will'. Every activity designed to promote proper human values was part of our response to the mission received through the Gospel.

• *The Church – sign and herald of God's love*

> The Church is the universal sacrament of salvation; she makes known the mystery of God's love for men and women and makes it present among them.[14]

Anyone who knows the history of the Church knows how true this statement has been. Through the centuries the Church has been the herald of God's love for men, women and children in their different needs. In various ways it has been the sign of God's compassionate love among us. However, this image of Christ's compassion on the face of the Church has not been totally untarnished. It has not always shone through clearly for others to see. In every age, we who are the Church must examine our conscience regarding the image that the Church projects through us.

To make a distinction that is theoretically questionable but practically true, the Church, through its official teachers, has seemed at times to be more concerned with the truth than with 'doing the truth in love'. A so-called concern for truth (more often for ways of formulating a truth) has seemed to exclude a true human and Christian charity. We have only to recall the Inquisition, the burning of heretics, and the recriminations of pre-ecumenical days to realise how true this is. There are modern ways of insisting on truth which seem to rule out compassion and love. The truth should help us to love. But who can grasp the whole truth? And how often has the so-called insistence on truth (and on law) destroyed real Christian charity? It is easy to appear uncaring for persons in a care for 'the truth'.

In so far as this is true of the Church in any age, to that extent has it failed in its mission to be the sacrament of Christ's love, compassionate and kind. Some failure is inevitable in this regard, for many adults are like children who regard any insistence on truth, or imposition of discipline as a failure to love.

True love is demanding. But its demands will be met in the measure that they are seen to be the demands of love. The Church must preach the truth. But the primordial truth of God's love for us all must be preached more loudly than all the rest. Furthermore, only those can truly preach God's truth who have learned to believe in this love and are people of compassionate hearts:

> While he (Jesus) was at dinner in the house, it happened that a number of tax collectors and sinners came to sit at the table with Jesus and his disciples. When the Pharisees saw this they said to his disciples: 'Why does your master eat with tax collectors and sinners?' When he heard this, he replied: 'It is not the healthy who need the doctor, but the sick. Go and learn the meaning of the words: *What I want is mercy, not sacrifice.* And indeed I did not come to call the virtuous but sinners' (Mt 9:10-15).

In accord with these words of Jesus, a basic truth that the Church must preach is that Jesus loves sinners – and tax collectors, and divorcees, and people who practise birth control. He wills to 'free them from sin by might of his great loving'. The Church proclaims Christ's love for every man and woman no matter what their situation, no matter what their way of acting. This is not to say that the Church thinks it does not matter what are our situations or our ways of acting. Some values it must constantly assert such as those of fidelity in marriage, reverence for human life. However, it does not brand as sinners those who do not live up to these values, or who do not accept that they are truly Christian values. The Church has taught: 'In the last analysis conscience is inviolable, and no one is forced to act contrary to conscience as the constant tradition of the Church attests.'[15]

Perhaps the Church would do well to preach from the housetops truths like this. For here, too, are truths which are part of the Gospel message of God's love for us. Some authorities are afraid that if we preach these truths loud and clear, we are in danger of setting double standards. Such is not the case. However, it is important, that like its Lord and Master, the Church shows that it 'loves with a human heart' – kind, compassionate and understanding of human weakness.

• *The Church and the kingdom of God*

Speaking of the kingdom of God, announced by Jesus, the Vatican Council said: 'Here on earth, the kingdom is already present in mystery. When the Lord returns, it will enter into its perfection'. And it is, of course, a 'kingdom of truth and life, a kingdom of holiness and grace, a kingdom of justice, love and peace'.[16]

The Church must promote the kingdom. The Council clearly stated that part of the Church's mission is to foster all that is truly human; to work that proper human values may be universally recognised and acted on. For the kingdom of God is present and developing wherever there is goodness, beauty, truth, love.

Vatican II spoke of wide fields of human endeavour in which Christians should work for the coming of the kingdom. Consequently when Christians ask what they should do as part of their Christian action, the choices are many. Each one should examine carefully personal gifts, inclination, possibilities presented – and then make a personal choice as how best to live one's

Christian vocation. And, of course, such action is part of one's Christian spiritual life inspired by the gospel.

Subsequently, Popes developed the Council's message about the Church's mission to promote the kingdom of God. Paul VI and John Paul II have both made significant statements on this topic. They sharpened the Church's vision. The Church does not exist for itself, they say; it exists that God's kingdom (of love and justice and peace) might come, partially in this world, fully in the next.

Pope Paul VI wrote:

> Christ first of all proclaimed a kingdom, the kingdom of God, and this is so important, that, by comparison, everything else becomes the rest which is given in addition. Only the kingdom therefore is absolute, and it makes everything else relative.[17]

God is at work in the world, working to establish a kingdom of love, justice and peace, in which the rights of every person are respected; in which healthy relations exist in families and in human society. By proclaiming the teachings of Christ and the human values which he extolled, 'the Church believes she can contribute much to make the human family and its history more human... and imbues the daily activity of people with a deeper sense and meaning.'[18]

The mission of the Church (and the mission of its members) is not primarily to convert people to Christianity, but to foster, witness to and promote the values of the kingdom. One important element of the Church's mission to the world is 'to affirm the special dignity of every human person which implies the defence and promotion of human rights'.[19]

The whole of the Church as such is directly called to the service of charity...charity towards one's neighbour through contemporary forms of the traditional spiritual and corporal works of mercy, represents the most immediate, ordinary and habitual ways that lead to the Christian animation of the temporal order... A charity that loves and serves the person is never able to be separated from justice.[20]

Here it is worth noting that there is a consistency, too, in the way the Church's mission unfolds. All that the Church is asked to do is one or other expression of love I have just quoted the Pope's statement that justice is a form of love. Today, care for the environment is a prime concern of many people. 'O Lord', wrote Tagore, 'let me feel this world as your love taking form, then my love will help it.'

Therefore, understandably, many Christians feel that it is their Christian duty to live out a concern for the environment – and the present Pope has written of our duty in this field.

Many a Christian will feel called to work for the 'Christian animation of the temporal order' by 'participating in public life' in 'faithful and unselfish dedication for the good of all'.[21] In particular, the 'lay faithful, having responsibilities in various capacities and at different levels of science as well as in the medical, social legislative and economic fields must *courageously accept the "challenge" posed by new problems in bioethics'*.[22] This is one element of the wider challenge to see that the culture in which we live is permeated, as much as possible, by Christian and human values.

Perhaps the clearest explanation of the relationship existing between Christ, Church and kingdom is given by Pope John Paul II in his encyclical letter, *Redemptoris missio*. It is worth reading:

> The Church serves the kingdom by spreading throughout the world the 'gospel values' which are an expression of the kingdom and help people to accept God's plan...the inchoate reality of the kingdom can also be found beyond the confines of the Church, among peoples everywhere to the extent that they live 'gospel values' and are open to the working of the Spirit who breathes where he wills (cf Jn 3:8). But it must immediately be added that this temporal dimension of the kingdom remains incomplete unless it is related to the kingdom of Christ present in the Church and straining towards eschatological fullness.
>
> ...The Church is the sacrament of salvation for all mankind and her activity is not limited only to those who accept her message. She is a dynamic force in mankind's journey towards the eschatological kingdom, and is the sign and promoter of gospel values. The Church contributes to mankind's pilgrimage towards conversion to God's plan through her witness, and through such activities as dialogue, human promotion, commitment to justice and peace, education and the care of the sick, and aid to the poor and to children. In carrying on these activities, however, she never loses sight of the priority of the transcendent and spiritual realities.
>
> Finally the Church serves the kingdom by her intercession, since the kingdom by its very nature is God's gift and work... We must ask for the kingdom, welcome it and make it grow within us. But we must also work together so that it will be welcomed and will grow among all people.[23]

• *The Church – a community of prayer and worship*

We have just been considering one of the ways in which the Church is 'a chosen race'. A second meaning of that phrase should be clear from a consideration of the full text from St Peter's letter: 'You are a chosen race, a royal priesthood, a consecrated nation, a people set apart to sing the praises of God who called you out of darkness into his own wonderful light' (1 Pet 2:9). Perhaps the Church is most truly Church and most evidently Church when it is, and is seen to be, a community called together by God to give thanks for gifts received, to sing God's praises, to listen to the Scriptures and to offer our lives to God.

Liturgy, Eucharist, sacraments and prayer are very much at the heart of any true Catholic spiritual life. The sacraments will be more strongly integrated into our spiritual lives if they reflect the vision we have of a loving God. This is why some of the references in the baptismal liturgy (to exorcism of evil spirits, to stain of sin, etc) jar on some people's ears. More consistent with our vision is Cardinal Martini's description of baptism:

Baptism is: entrusting ourselves to God's loving plan; joining the Church, which is the hope of the world. For each of us baptism marks the Father's embrace. It is an effective sign of vital relationships which the Father, Son and Spirit share with us. It gives us a new heart. It enables us to obey filially – like Jesus – God's plan.

Baptism marks our entrance into the great family that is the Church. It enables us to celebrate the Eucharist, to hear and witness the Word of the Lord, to live fraternal charity, and to put our gifts at the service of all.

Finally, baptism makes us a sign of hope for all humanity, because it makes us a new humanity freed from sin, ready to enter into the many ways of human living, but not with aggressive egoism that demands everything selfishly, but with firm openness to be drawn by Christ and disposed to help, celebrate, serve and love.[24]

Every sacrament is, in its own way, a symbol of God's embracing love.

When considering the Church and the kingdom of God, we listed a number of ways in which Christians should work to make the world a better place. However, as members of the People of God, each of us has to remember St Paul's words: 'Each one of us, however, has been given our own share of grace, given as Christ allotted it... And to some his gift was that they should be apostles, to some prophets; to some evangelists, to some pastors and teachers...so that the saints together make a unity in the work of service building up the body of Christ' (Eph 4:7,11-13).

How am I being called to exercise a special role in the Church for the building up of the Body of Christ?

• *Mary, mother of the Church*

Mary has a special place in the gospels. She was the mother of the saviour: 'And your own soul a sword shall pierce' (Lk 2:35). She walked with Jesus to Calvary, she drank the woman's cup:

> She has trodden all the paths of our human existence,
> she has gone through the darkness and the suffering,
> through the abyss of loneliness and pain.

Devotion to Mary has always been part of the Catholic spiritual tradition. However, its expression varies from one culture to another, from one person to another. The Second Vatican Council asked for a balanced and healthy devotion 'proceeding from true faith' refraining from 'false exaggerations' and 'vain credulity'.[25] Each has to find the special place that Mary has in his or her life. This truth is beautifully expressed in the following passage from a little book called *Rule for a New Brother.*

> Mary will have her own place in your life.
> You cannot separate her from the Lord
> who chose her as his mother and his bride.
>
> She is the selfless space
> where God became man;
> She is the silence in which God's Word can be heard.
> She is the free woman, subject to none,
> not even to the powers of evil.
>
> She is the image of the Church,
> Her self-effacing service will guide you to the Lord.
> Her faith and fidelity
> are a model for your life.
>
> She has trodden all the paths
> of our human existence;
> she has gone through darkness and suffering,
> through the abyss of loneliness and pain.
>
> She is the little creature
> through whom God's grandeur shines out;
> she is the poor one
> filled with divine riches.
> She is wholly grace,
> and grace for you.
>
> Then take your part joyfully
> in the prophecy of Scripture:
> 'Behold henceforth all generations
> will call me blessed.'[26]

A time for all things under the sun

We must always remember that Jesus thought of the kingdom in terms of a feast. A gloomy Christian is a contradiction in terms. Locke, the great philosopher defined laughter as 'a sudden glory'. There is no healthy pleasure that is forbidden to a Christian...for a Christian is like someone who is forever at a wedding feast.[27]

According to the book of Ecclesiastes (3:1-8), there is a time for all things under the sun – a time to plant and a time to pluck up what is planted, a time to dance and a time to mourn. There is 'a time to laugh and a time to weep'. There is also a *way* to use all things under the sun. The healthy human way is also the way of God, creator and giver of all good things – and our strength and help in hard times.

St Augustine has a fine formula for the way in which we should use God's gifts:

> If material things please you, then praise God for them but turn back your love upon him who made them...If souls please you then love them in God. The good that you love is from him; and in so far as it is likewise *for* him, it is good and lovely; but it will be rightly turned into bitterness if it is unrightly loved and he deserted by whom it is.[28]

And since there is a time to give free rein to reflection, let me add that there is also a way to laugh and a way to weep. In Mark 5:40 'they laughed at him' – they laughed at Jesus, those who did not know the power that would raise a dead girl to life. In Luke 23:37, 'they wept for him' – those women who had begun to glimpse his goodness. The laughter was their loss; the weeping was their gain.

Laughter closes your eyes, and makes you blind to all that you could discover in the one you laugh *at*. Yet laughter can also open your eyes to see, provided you laugh *with* the one you are prepared to love. In such laughter you can see the world anew, lit with the smile of God.

Compassion will open your eyes even as they fill with tears, for compassion opens the heart. Whenever you weep from sorrow, loss or pain, know that he weeps with you who wept for Lazarus, for Jerusalem and all the cities of the earth. But you weep alone whenever, in anger or resentment, you weep bitter tears. These, too, close your eyes even as they close your heart.

The cup we drink

Touched as they are by the splendour of divine love, ours are still very human lives. Each will have its own share of suffering and pain. As men and women, we are called to drink the cup of our own human weakness. As followers of Christ, we drink it in union with him.

> As the Son, He (Jesus) chooses between following a life without the Father, and accepting death with the Father. He chooses obedience. He chooses the Father's will, being with him to the end...When the Christian chooses to give his or her life, to serve others, to take up the cross, to wash the feet of his or her fellow human being, to accept a life transformed by the Gospel, to accept the requirements that life brings at home, at work, in school and in society, when he or she accepts the suffering that is part of this life, and the solitude akin to Christ's that comes with it - that Christian does not do so out of some strange desire to suffer, but because he or she has discovered the face of the Father, and has understood that the spring of life is found in doing the Father's will, even when that indicates a road of sacrifice and dedication unto death.[29]

In the next chapter we shall see how Mary MacKillop – Sister Mary of the Cross – can serve as our model and teacher, as we are faced with human suffering and trials.

Personal prayer

Our spiritual lives begin with faith in a God who loves us. This love is sheer grace, gift of God poured forth in our hearts by the Holy Spirit who is given to us. The grateful acknowledgment of these truths is itself a prayer as we open our minds and hearts to the Spirit of God.

Faith and prayer are bound together. A living faith naturally expresses itself in prayer; faith needs to be nourished by prayer if it is to remain alive. Prayer is very much a matter of individual choice and personal taste. However, there are some ways of praying which should be part of everyone's prayer life – such as the *Our Father*, the prayer that Jesus taught us. One of the oldest forms of prayer is called *lectio divina* or 'divine reading' – a prayerful reading of Scripture.

> The Church recommends the reading of the Word of God as a source of Christian prayer, and at the same time exhorts all to discover the deep meaning of Sacred Scripture through prayer.[30]

In the Bible, too, we find one of the easiest and most natural ways of praying – the 'eucharistic' prayer. We all know that 'eucharist' comes from a Greek word meaning 'to give thanks' and for many Catholics it has come to be identified with the Mass. But eucharistic prayers existed long before Jesus and generally they contained four steps in an easy and natural method of prayer:

1. The eucharistic prayer begins with a 'calling to mind'. We recall all that God has done for us – 'the wonderful works of God'. It is most moving to take part in prayer sessions in some countries where the people are very poor. A superficial observer would say that they have nothing for which to give thanks. Yet they spend quite some time in thanking God – for life, for health, for love, for Jesus Christ and all that he has done for us. Then we begin to understand why St Paul so stressed the value of gratitude for the spiritual life.

2. Having recalled what God has done for us, we pass naturally to the further steps of praising the goodness of God, and giving thanks for all that God has done.

3. Furthermore, as we call to mind God's blessings, we are filled with confidence and trust: 'So long thy power hath blessed me sure it still will lead me on'.[31]

4. We then come to the final part of the eucharistic prayer. As we have called to mind God's blessings, we ask God to keep in mind all the blessed, to watch over us and to help us in our need.

Some prayers, which we learned in childhood, may need to be changed as our theological vision changes. For example, the act of faith that I learned went something like this: 'O my God, I believe all that Thou hast taught because Thou art truth itself. I believe all that the Catholic Church believes and teaches'. In itself, there is merit in this prayer. However, an act of faith flowing more naturally from the vision of God's love would run something like this: 'O my God, I believe in your love, the love that gave me life, the love that redeemed me, the love that guides me.'

Time given to prayer will vary from one person to another. Cardinal Newman gave some advice on prayer which is still very practical today:

> Watch and pray and meditate, that is, according to the leisure which God has given you. Give freely of your time to your Lord and Saviour, if you have it. If you have little, show your sense of the privilege by giving that little. But any how show that your heart and desires, show that your life, is with your God. Set aside every day times for seeking him.... I am not calling on you to go out of the world or to abandon your duties in the world, but to redeem the time; not to give hours to mere amusement or society, while you give minutes to Christ.[32]

Taste varies, too, from one person to another. I presume to quote a few prayers that appeal to me. The first three come from the Breviary:

Lord God, in your wisdom you created us,
by your providence you rule us;
penetrate our inmost being with your holy light,
so that our way of life may always be one of faithful service to you.

Let your people's cry come into your loving presence, Lord,
Forgive them their sins,
so that by your grace they may be devoted to your service
and rest secure under your protecting hand.

Our heart's desire to love Thee, Lord,
watch over while we sleep.

From the Mass for Australia Day comes an inspiring
Australian prayer:

God, powerful and gentle,
You love this southern land
and all its peoples, old and new.
As the Cross shines in our heavens
so may Christ bring light to our nation,
as the waves encircle our shores
so may your mercy enfold us all.

May the God who formed our southern land
be for us a rock of strength.
May the God who rules our southern seas
keep us safe in every storm.
May the God who made our southern skies
turn our darkness into light.

Those looking for a prayer to the Holy Spirit, could
hardly do better than the Canberra meeting of the
World Council of Churches which proposed this prayer:

Spirit of light: let your wisdom shine on us.
Spirit of silence: make us aware of God's presence.
Spirit of courage: dispel the fear in our hearts.
Spirit of fire: inflame us with Christ's love.
Spirit of peace: help us to be still and listen to God's Word.
Spirit of joy: inspire us to proclaim the Good News.
Spirit of love: help us to open ourselves to the needs of others.

Spirit of power: give us your help and your strength.
Spirit of truth: guide us in the way of Christ. Amen.

The *Catechism of the Catholic Church* reminds us that 'the life of prayer is the habit of being in the presence of the thrice-holy God and in communion with him.'[33] One well-known prayer that stresses the presence of God is this:

Christ be with me, Christ within me,
Christ behind me, Christ before me,
Christ beside me, Christ to win me,
Christ to comfort and restore me.
Christ beneath me, Christ above me,
Christ in quiet, Christ in danger,
Christ in hearts of all that love me,
Christ in mouth of friend and stranger.

Presence of God

God 'chose us, chose us in Christ, to be holy and spotless, and to live through love in his presence' (Eph 1: 4).

On more than one occasion Mary MacKillop wrote that she 'did not pray much'. She would then go on to add 'but feel calm and tranquil and near our dear good God',[34] or 'God's presence seems to follow me everywhere and make everything I do, or wish to do, a prayer'.[35] There has never been a saint who thought she prayed enough. But Mary's Sisters had a quite different version of the way she prayed: 'In prayer she would stay up for hours praying. I have known her to stay up frequently for a couple of hours praying.'[36] 'She was always praying when I was a Novice. She was always a woman of prayer.'[37]

It is a pity that Mary did not have a chance to read the recent *Catechism of the Catholic Church*. She would have been happy to find there the teaching, just cited, which is true for many busy people who desire to serve God: 'The life of prayer is the habit of being in the presence of the thrice-holy God and in communion with him.' This statement expresses an old tradition in the Church, for example:

> The prayer I have in mind... is not tied down to a fixed timetable; rather it is a state of mind which endures by night and day. Our soul should be directed in God, not merely when we suddenly think of prayer, but even when we are concerned with something else. If we are looking after the poor, if we are busy in some other way, or if we are doing any type of good work, we should season our actions with the desire and remembrance of God.[38]

Mary MacKillop's sense of the presence of God is consistent with a vision of a loving and caring God: 'Many things...might discourage were it not for a certain sense of God's watchful love.'[39]

Clearly, in the spiritual life we should try to develop this habit of being in the presence of God's watchful love. Not that we are always thinking of God; but 'though your tongue is silent, your heart speaks aloud. God has ears for what our heart is saying.'[40]

For many people, the beauty of nature speaks to them clearly of the presence of God; contemplation of the wonder of creation is part of their prayer.

> Look upon the rainbow and praise its maker,
> exceedingly beautiful in its brightness.
> It encircles the heavens with its glorious arc;
> the hands of the most high have stretched it out.
> (Ecclesiasticus [Sirach] 43:11-12)

The psalms

'Prayed and fulfilled in Christ, the psalms are an essential and permanent element of the prayer of the Church. They are suitable for men and women of every condition and time.'[41] The Church has her own way of praying the psalms during Mass and in the Liturgy of the Hours. Individuals differ in their appreciation of the psalms as personal prayer. One good way to pray the psalms is to look for passages that appeal to you and to reflect on those passages, expanding them into personal prayers of your own. They are, after all, filled with love and trust and hope.

For example, Psalm 118:77 says: 'Let your love come upon me Lord and I shall live'. This can be expanded: 'Lord, your love came upon us to give us life; your love came in baptism to make us children of God. Your love came and we were called on the way of love. Your love comes in many ways, and at the last your love will come upon us that we might live. Then "you will give me the fullness of joy in your presence, O Lord, I will find happiness at your right hand forever"' (Ps 16:11).

Psalm 103 lends itself to prayerful reflection:

High are the heavens over the earth.
Can you measure the height?
Can you measure God's love?
How deep the compassion,
how far-reaching the love.
The Lord is compassion and love
embracing earth and heaven,
extending beyond the stars.

Another passage that can provide food for reflection comes from Psalm 92:

I will sing of your love in the morning
and of fidelity when evening comes.

Let us sing of love every morning, of God's love that gave us life, of Christ's love as he gave his life that we might live forever, forever to sing of God's love. If we sing of God's love in the morning, we will give thanks when evening comes for God's fidelity that kept us faithful. 'I thank you for your faithfulness and love that excel all we ever knew of you' (Ps 138).

I will sing of your love at midday and in the afternoon,
when the heat is harsh and the burden heavy,
and beauty hidden by the haze.
Even then – especially then – must I trust in your love
if I am to be faithful till evening comes.
And when evening does come at last
I will sing of your faithfulness
if I can still sing of your love – only if I still sing of your love.

---

1 John Paul II, *Apostolic Exhortation on the Vocation and Mission of the Lay Faithful in the Church and in the World (Christifideles laici)*, 1989, n 11.

2 St Augustine, *Confessions* 2,X.

3 *Christifideles laici*, n 59.

4 Vatican II, *Dogmatic Constitution on the Church (Lumen gentium)*, n 34.

5 John Kavanaugh, *The Word Embodied*, p 14.

6 *Lumen gentium*, n 48; Vatican II, *Decree on the Church's Missionary Activity (Ad gentes)*, n 1,5.

7 *Lumen gentium*, n 1.

8 E J Cuskelly, *No Cowards in the Kingdom*, Melbourne: Spectrum, 1969, pp 53-4.

9 K Rahner, 'The Cloister of the Future', *Herder Correspondence* Vol 2 No 7 (1965), pp 207-12.

10 Cuskelly, *No Cowards*, p 57.

11 *Lumen gentium*, n 16.

12 Vatican II, *Pastoral Constitution on the Church in the Modern World* (*Gaudium et spes*), n 45.

13 Pontifical Council for Promoting Christian Unity, *Directory for the Application of the Principles and Norms of Ecumenism*, 1993, n 9.

14 *Gaudium et spes*, n 45.

15 Sacred Congregation for the Clergy, Document in the 'Washington Case', 1970, in A Flannery (ed), *Vatican Council II: More Postconciliar Documents*, Vol 2, Dublin: Dominican Publications, 1982, p 420.

16 *Gaudium et spes*, n 39.

17 Paul VI, *Apostolic exhortation on Evangelisation in the Modern World* (*Evangelii nuntiandi*), 1975, n 8.

18 *Gaudium et spes*, n 40.

19 *Christifideles laici*, n 39.

20 *Ibid*, n 41-2.

21 *Ibid*, n 42.

22 *Ibid*, n 38.

23 John Paul II, *Encyclical letter on the Permanent Validity of the Church's Missionary Mandate* (*Redemptoris missio*), 1991, n 20.

24 C M Martini, *Journeying with the Lord: Reflections for every day*, New York: Alba House, 1987, pp 74-5.

25 *Lumen gentium*, n 67.

26 H van der Looy, *Rule for a New Brother*, translated by the Benedictine Nuns of Cockfosters, London: Darton, Longman and Todd, 1973, pp 52-3.

27 W Barclay, *The Gospel of Luke* (rev ed), Edinburgh: St Andrew's Press, 1975, p 195.

28 *Confessions*, 4,XII.

29 Martini, *Journeying*, p 43.

30 Congregation for the Doctrine of the Faith, *Letter to the Bishops of the Catholic Church on Some Aspects of Christian Meditation*, 1989, n 6.

31 J H Newman, *Lead, Kindly Light*.

32 Newman, Sermon 15, 'Rising with Christ', in *Parochial and Plain Sermons, Vol VI*, London: Longmans, Green and Co, 1907, pp 208-20.

33 *Catechism of the Catholic Church*, Homebush: St Pauls Publications, 1994, n 2565.

34 *MacKillop Letterbook*, MacKillop to Woods, 19 September 1871, Mary MacKillop Archives, North Sydney.

35 *Letterbook*, MacKillop to Woods, 28 March 1870.

36 Testimony of Mother Laurence O'Brien, *Positio Super Causae Introductione*, process 11, ad 4, in Positio Super Viritutibus, Rome 1989, p 29.

37 Testimony of Sister Isabel, *Ibid*, process 10, ad 3.

38 St John Chrysostom, Homily 6 *On Prayer.*

39 *Letterbook*, MacKillop to the Sisters, Feast of the Annunciation 1883.

40 St Augustine, *On Psalm 48.*

41 *Catechism of the Catholic Church*, n 2597.

Bishop James Cuskelly MSC
1924-1999

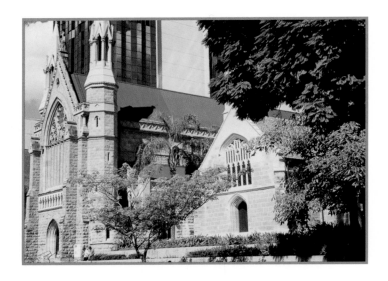

The 1850 Chapel of St Stephen (above) beside St Stephen's Cathedral, Brisbane.

The apse of this recently restored and renovated Chapel has been dedicated as a diocesan shrine to Mary MacKillop.

Left: interior of St Stephen's Chapel.

Image and quotes of Blessed Mary MacKillop
inscribed on wooden planks that divide
the Mary MacKillop shrine from the liturgical space
in St Stephen's Chapel, Brisbane.

Blessed Mary MacKillop.
Wood sculpture by John Elliott,
St Stephen's Chapel, Brisbane.

Created from pieces of the trunk of an old camphor laurel tree,
the figure evokes the tough pioneering spirit of this holy
woman. Her faith and trust in God's providence are shown in
her determination as she strides forward. Yet her face tells of her
warmth and compassion for those in need.

4

Mary MacKillop —
a spiritual model for Australasia

There are some actions which should be seen as rich in symbolism. For us in Brisbane one such action is the renovation of the old St Stephen's Cathedral and its consecration as a shrine of Blessed Mary MacKillop. The symbolism is twofold:

Firstly, the old cathedral was the heart of the spiritual life of the Brisbane Church, and its restoration and reopening in February 1999 is a symbol of a renewal of the spiritual life which should flourish in the Archdiocese.

Secondly, its dedication as a shrine of Blessed Mary MacKillop is the expression of a hope that, in her life and example, all of us will find inspiration to live as true disciples of Jesus, walking his way, telling his truth, living his life.

Mary MacKillop was beatified by Pope John Paul II on 19 January, 1995. The beatification was a declaration that she was a woman who had walked the way of Jesus, told his truth and lived his life. The Pope also declared that she was a model for the rest of us who live in these lands. Her spirituality should serve as inspiration to us. In describing her vision and response, the Pope said (in words similar to ones we have already used):

> Mother Mary's life speaks eloquently because it was firmly anchored in something which every human heart longs for: inner peace, that peace that comes from knowing that one is loved by God and from the desire to respond to his love. She knew that God loved her and she did not doubt; freely and unassumingly she responded to this love with confidence and courage.[1]

The way of Jesus, which Mary MacKillop walked, can be described as follows:

1. It was a way walked in God's presence. 'He who sent me is with me' (Jn 16:32).
2. It entailed preaching the Good News to the poor (Lk 4:18).
3. It was the way of God's will. 'My food is to do the will of the One who sent me' (Jn 4:34).
4. It was the way of the cross (Heb 12:2).
5. It was the way of love and forgiveness (Jn 15:12; Lk 6:37).
6. It was in loving one's enemies (Mt 5:43-48).

Let us now see how Mary MacKillop walked this way.

She lived in God's presence

> I have never felt such calm – such a sense of the Presence, the sweet Presence of God, as I have done since I left you at the Port station just before we parted. I may say that it has never left me, it makes everything that is hard, easy. I just get a taste of bitterness in some things and then something calm and soft raises my mind above it all. I feel this

Presence of God at all times – when talking to old friends, strangers, the Sisters or the Priests. Sometimes it comes, Oh so beautifully after a little struggle with something that I do not like to do. It makes me see God – His Holy Will and immense mercy in everything.[2]

She brought the Good News to the poor.

In the Mary MacKillop shrine in Brisbane, John Elliott's statue of Mary is the statue of a woman walking, a woman striding forth to do God's will, to answer the cry of the poor. The driving force in her life was the need to respond to the needs of poor children in the Australian colonies. She worked at this mission generously, heroically 'telling his truth', teaching the truths of the Christian faith to those who, without her and her Sisters, would not know the teachings of Christ. Still in her later years, this concern for the poor shines forth – 'Let others seek the more remarkable places, but let St Joseph's true children remember their mission and seek first the poorest, most neglected parts of God's vineyard.'[3]

She and her Sisters worked for poor children and their parents, for girls in trouble, for orphans, for jailbirds - for the poor wherever she found them and could bring them help. 'No doubt its principal work is the education of children, but the Rule expressly says "That the Sisters must do all the good they can, and never see an evil without trying to discover how they may remedy it".'[4]

She walked the way of God's will

She wrote somewhere: 'And behind it all <u>God's Will</u> (underlining hers) to be done by us, God's Will to be accepted in all that comes to us.' [5]

To her mother, she wrote: 'Your submission to the Will of God, your resignation under affliction, and your always confiding simple trust in Divine Providence proved a wonderful comfort and example to me...and poor dear Papa, too. I was not long in religion when I clearly saw how much I owed to him.'[6]

In an article entitled *Mary MacKillop and the Will of God* Margaret Paton writes:

> The will of God was THE formative influence in her being to which she joyfully yielded herself, body, mind and spirit. But there was nothing weak or passive about her attitude. She had a rich sense of the will of God at work in the circumstances, events and persons of her life. When troubles came, as they did in plenty, she looked at them creatively to find concealed in them the will of God for her at the particular time and in the particular circumstances in which she found herself...the will of God was rooted in Mary MacKillop's make-up. It was a lens through which she could make sense of whatever happened in her life. The difficulties that she encountered were never just adverse circumstances; they were the new shape of what a loving God was bringing into being.[7]

'The new shape of what a loving God was bringing into being,' her 'simple trust in the Divine Providence' of a loving God was woven through her search for God's will as well as her acceptance of the cross. Hers was a 'consistent vision' of a loving God at work in the world and present in every circumstance of her life.[8]

Even though they do not always formulate all the implications of their spiritual insights, the saints state certain truths which we can develop further. Connected with Mary MacKillop's insistence on the importance of our accepting God's will, is a truth that is very important for every spiritual life. Each of us is called to enter into the paschal mystery of Jesus – passing through death to self to share in his risen life. This will mean that, in fact, at some stage of our lives (or at a number of stages) each of us will have to pass through an experience like that of Jesus in Gethsemane. Life will not go the way we expected or wanted. Then we must choose; either we rebel – or we pray: 'Not my will, but thine be done'. And we must choose further how we pray.

Some people, at times, offer what is no more than a half-resentful prayer: 'Thy will be done'. But, if we take a closer look at the Gospel we see that Jesus' prayer was: 'Father, *Abba*, dear Father, thy will be done'. Only this prayer of Jesus would be Mary MacKillop's prayer; and it alone is a fruitful prayer.

After Gethsemane, Jesus took a further step in accepting God's will when he was crucified. As he was nailed to the cross, he prayed: 'Father forgive them'. As he died, he said 'Father into your hands I commend my spirit.' Fr Bede Jarrett OP wrote some beautiful reflections on these last words on the cross. He pointed out that those who watched saw only the cruel hands of the soldiers who nailed Jesus to the cross. However, Jesus himself, behind the human hands, saw his Father's hands and prayed: 'Father forgive; into your hands...' Jarrett goes on to say: so often in life other people hurt you, at times your friends, your superiors. When that happens, he asks, can you go as far as Jesus? Can you see, behind the hands that hurt you, can you see your Father's hands? Can you accept, can you forgive? Mary MacKillop could, which is one reason that she is Blessed.

She went the way of the cross

Mary MacKillop became Sister Mary of the Cross. On 21 August, 1867 she wrote to her mother: 'If we could only remember that we are placed here to suffer and that God may be glorified under the smallest as well as the greatest trials, much that would otherwise be difficult would become easy'.[9]

> My name in Religion is Mary of the Cross. No name could be dearer to me, so I must endeavour, not to deserve it - for I cannot - but at least I must try not to disgrace it... [10]

> I am far happier than one who bears the name of the Cross should be, but then every trouble ceases to be one when I think of that name. [11]

Today many, many people think that life should be a 'living happily ever after' in this life. When that does not happen they blame God for not bringing it about. Mary did not think that way. She thought that suffering and trials were a normal to-be-expected part of human existence. She also thought that those trials and sufferings were used by a loving God for our own good and the good of others. Further, she saw that suffering and the Cross were part of the life of Jesus. Therefore, the Cross would be part of the life of the followers of Christ. Consequently, no cross could make her unhappy.

SISTER MARY OF THE CROSS. Behind the acceptance of this name, was a well thought out personal spirituality. She was a woman of her times; and what Margaret Paton wrote of her thinking about the will of God would also apply to her way of thinking and speaking about the cross: 'Her approach...was to some extent conditioned by nineteenth century spirituality which differs from a twentieth century approach'.[12] We would have some difficulty with the way in which she envisages God freely sending us crosses for our spiritual good. Nevertheless, her teaching is sound, including these elements:

• 'The Cross (trials and sufferings) will be present in each human life.'[13]

• 'How you cope with the cross spells your success or failure as a human being and as a Christian.'[14]

• 'The way to cope should go beyond mere resignation.'[15]

• 'Faith is the first essential if we are to cope with the cross in life...faith in God as a loving Father who (if you let him) will, in his Providence, use trials and sufferings for your greater good and his *glory*.'[16] 'Every sorrow that he sends is intended to convey some special blessing to our souls.'[17] '...faith in Jesus who carried his Cross for love of us.'[18]

> 'The more closely you strive to follow Christ, the more will the Cross be present in your life – in the way of extra renunciation.'[19]

She walked the way of love and forgiveness

An Italian Cardinal, who may know very little about Mary MacKillop, in fact described her perfectly when he wrote:

> The faithful adult Christian can be described as the person who allows himself or herself to be stretched to the fullest in *the exercise of charity*. It is only this perfect expansion of charity which provides the complete image of the Christian adult... The New Testament...says... 'Be imitators of God as his children, full of love, goodness, meekness, esteem for one another, and centered and supported by charity.'[20]

People will differ as to where they see true holiness in Mary MacKillop. It might be in her deep faith, her trust in God, her persevering courage, or her compassionate concern for the poor, especially the children. Certainly all of these things go to make up the total picture of the sanctity that was hers. For me the most striking manifestation of true holiness is to be found in her beautiful and heroic response to unfair and unjust treatment that she received. I marvel at the serenity, the sweet charity, the total respect for priesthood and her belief in the goodness of the motives of those who treated her so unfairly.

Most people would have been destroyed by similar treatment. Many people endeavour to justify themselves as they grow angry, or bitter or disillusioned when they believe they are treated badly or unfairly. In their anger, their bitterness, their disillusion they stop on the road to holiness. Some of them leave the Church. Others doubt God. Few, very few, go on unscarred for to do so requires a veritable miracle of grace. The purely human reaction is to be angry, vindictive, embittered. Only the saints walk on serene, never doubting that, even in the dark places, a loving God walks with them and that 'all manner of things will be well'. Only the saints can see, behind the hands that hurt them, the gentle hands of a loving Father. And only the saints succeed in thinking and speaking with loving charity of those who have acted badly towards them.

Mary is a wonderful example of someone whose faith and love were unshaken by her experience of the human poverty of the Church. One of the elements of heroic sanctity present in the life of Mary MacKillop was her unwavering faith in the Church. She met with its poverty in high places – in unworthy priests, in weak and arrogant bishops, in foolish nuns. Yet she never weakened in her faith in Christ present in and acting through the Church. Nothing lessened her resolve to go on working for the poor. The limitations of other members of the Church did not surprise or discourage her. She believed in the Church of the poor.

The sad happening of her excommunication came about through the hatred that one man, Fr Horan, had for Fr Tenison Woods. Horan was later expelled from the diocese. But before then, for personal, unworthy reasons he had built up a hatred for Woods. It was a blind hatred that had no concern for the harm it might do to others as long as Woods perished in the barrage launched against him. One of the ways of discrediting Woods was to discredit the religious congregation he had founded. This Horan set out to do, aided and abetted by one or other priest he had rallied to his cause. At the same time he would reshape the congregation according to his own ideas.

Woods had left himself open to attack. He had incurred debts for himself and his congregation – many were unpaid. He was a 'sucker' for supernatural phenomena and had believed in some alleged experiences and visions of two of the Sisters, which were really quite strange and eventually proved to be a hoax. Thus Horan had ample ammunition to convince an old and ailing bishop that something had to be done to set right the affairs of the Sisters founded by Fr Tenison Woods and Sr Mary MacKillop.

Things could be put in order, Horan suggested, by making some changes to the Rule under which, up till now, the Sisters operated. Firstly, since not all were equally well educated, let them be divided into two classes (as many other congregations were) of choir (educated nuns who would teach) and lay (uneducated) Sisters. Secondly, let the Sisters – all of them – be subject, not to any central religious authority within the congregation, but to the local parish priest of the parish in which they worked.

The first of these provisions ran counter to all Mary's ideas of simplicity and community. The second was a recipe for disaster. With due deference, she informed the bishop that such a Rule was not the one she had taken her vows to observe, nor was it one which she was prepared to observe in the future. So, respectfully, she informed the bishop, that either the Rule stayed as it was, or she would not stay in a religious congregation with that sort of revamped Rule. She was quite right, of course (and had taken the trouble to be well advised on the issue). But Horan cried *disobedience*, fabricated a lie or two and prevailed upon the bishop to excommunicate Mary MacKillop.

It was some months before the excommunication was lifted – by a dying and repentant bishop. During those months, Mary was helped and supported by a number of people who realised how mistaken the bishop had been. A number of these were good lay people, some of them Protestant, one of them a generous Jewish gentleman. There was also a group of the priests, especially the Jesuits, who proved themselves 'sincere and fearless friends'.[21] These were the ones who sensed that, no matter what might be said or done by some priests, and the bishop influenced by them, Mary was a woman in whom the gospel had come alive.

Mary had a realistic view of the members of the Church – and of her own congregation: 'Let us work together and bear with one another. We all have faults. No one is perfect amongst us.'[22] There is a touch of humour in the way she points out that our faults can affect others: 'Remember that we must always expect from time to time to receive crosses, and know that we also give them.'[23]

The beauty and the strength of Mary MacKillop's holiness shines through her reaction to the excommunication imposed (unjustly) on her by Bishop Sheil. Not a word of bitterness, no resentment, in spite of the hurt, for deep hurt there surely was. And with the hurt, too, the urge to anger as there always is when we experience injustice.

> Nothing that happened to myself or the Sisters was hard enough to disturb my peace.
>
> I felt the greatest love for those who were persecuting us.[24]
>
> I can only remember dimly the things that were said to me, but the sensation of the calm, beautiful presence of God I shall never forget. [25]
>
> Once, though, I am sorry to say, that I felt anger – bitter and deep – or anguish rather at some terrible thing I heard.

Once she felt anger, but her anger turned to anguish as she suffered for another. And, of Sheil she would write – in proposing her Rule to Rome: 'The Rule in itself as approved by the late and much loved Bishop.' [26]

For Mary to get to this level of holiness or virtue she had to have acquired already a number of convictions:

• That God is a loving Father. Nothing could shake this conviction nor the consequent belief that good things are God's gift – for our good.

- Bad things, likewise, are 'His gift, in his wonderful Providence also working to our good'.[27] 'It would be a lack of faith, of trust, for us to fear that "bad things", allowed as they are by a loving God, can be for our ill.'[28]

- We would be wasting opportunities for personal growth and for furthering the cause of Christ *not* to take up the cross with love when it comes our way; not to see in it 'the sweet presence of God'.[29]

- Mary had taken the Gospel seriously. She had taken seriously the Lord's command *You shall love your neighbour as yourself.* Therefore, she believed in the goodness of people – she believed that they could be mistaken more often than malicious.[30] Always they merited respect. How many of us can say that we have really practised the Lord's words: 'Love your enemies, do good to those who hate you'? (Mt 5:44).

There are many examples of Mary's heroic way of thinking good of others, of loving those who treated her with disdain if not with enmity. One such example is Dr Cani in Brisbane. Bishop Quinn being away from the diocese, Dr Cani was in charge but the Sisters found him anything but cooperative. Mary wrote to Woods:

We have not seen Dr Cani, either, nor heard from him. Our dear Lord is permitting him to try us in this way. I am sure that willingly Dr Cani would not so try us. It is all the will of God and we are quite content. [31]

Dr Cani has been here to hear our confessions, the first time for a month. I mention the time not because I blame him. He is too good to have left us so long without cause.[32]

Dr Cani is really too good to wish to interfere with our Rule. [33]

Discussing this wonderful charity of Mary MacKillop, I have heard people say how hard they have found it to forgive others. Mary did not often forgive – for she did not often judge that people had need of forgiveness. She had a greater charity than that as forgiving presupposes the judgment that someone has done wrong and needs to be forgiven. Mary seldom made the judgment that someone had done wrong; she attributed good motives to them, believed that even wrongful actions were excused because of the ignorance, misconceptions or powerlessness of other people. This was the deeper charity which, believing good of others, found in them nothing that needed forgiving. For instance:

> This is the place for us to be well-exercised in mutual patience, charitable constructions and the like. We had not Mass here until Wednesday and I used to hear rather painful remarks about why Dr Cani did not keep his promises, why he did not come regularly to hear our Confessions – but they were more thoughtless than really heartfelt. Poor Dr. Cani could not help it. He has so much to do, and his lame foot is a great trouble to him....[34]
>
> 'I never doubt but that Dr Cani acts purely as he sees best.' [35]

Mary MacKillop put into practice a text of St Paul to which most of us could give further consideration: 'Love... is always ready to excuse, to trust, to hope' (1 Cor 13: 3).

> Sisters Augustine and Teresa are always the same - cheerful, good-natured and happy.[36]
>
> My poor Sisters are so good.[37]

But her belief in the goodness of her Sisters does not prevent her from correcting their faults in no uncertain terms: 'I often have to talk to her and have sometimes been forced to mortify her before the others.'[38] But there is no malice in these corrections: 'It gave me such a pang to inflict pain on one I loved so much for her gentleness.' [39]

She very much wanted charity to reign in the convents of her order:

> ...the feeling of sisterly love and union which should reign
> amongst us. Ah, my Sisters, let us love, let us cherish this
> beautiful feeling which will make our Convent home a lit-
> tle heaven on earth to us. Storms and persecution may rage
> around us; want, real biting want may stare us in the face,
> unkindness and humiliations of all kinds assail us, but in
> the Convent where Sisters dwell together in the holy bond
> of religion, nothing but love and charity should reign.[40]

That was her positive vision. When charity did not
reign she was not happy:

> There was such a lack of unity in the recreation last
> evening that I felt really angry and told the Sisters that I
> could not stay in the room. I went to the Oratory where
> some of them followed and seemed really contrite. In a
> few moments, I felt peace again there and went back.[41]

Her wide charity extended to nuns of other Religious
Orders, of whom she always wrote with esteem and
admiration.[42] She knew nothing of rivalry or jealousy,
but delighted in the good in others.

To her own Sisters she wrote:

> 'Bear with one another, help one another, construe
> charitably one another's actions, judge not, leaving that
> most painful duty to those appointed for it.'[43]

> 'He (God) looks to the motive, which man too often
> neglects to do.' [44]

It was because she looked to the motive, and because
(unless she had strong evidence to the contrary) she
presumed that people acted from good motives according to their lights, that she rarely felt the need to forgive.
To judge that you need to forgive is to judge that others
need forgiveness. This Mary would seldom do. She does

not forgive the bishop who excommunicated her. 'The poor Bishop has been our friend and would be so still, but there are some about him whom God permits to be bitterly opposed to Fr Woods and in a manner to myself.'[45]

But she does feel the need to forgive some of the priests:

> ...our poor dear Sisters feel that they are in the hands of bitter enemies instead of those of loved pastors. The poor dear gentlemen, from my heart I forgive them everything, but grieve to think that I have seen what I have seen or heard what I have heard.[46]

> Remember, Fr Horan is not to be trusted. I am willing to suffer in silence and take any blame upon myself, to be banished I care not where, but I cannot be silent if, by such, any priest who has defended the cause or in any way befriended us, will be made to suffer... You know how I venerate the priestly character, therefore you can understand what I have suffered since I have had to admit that a priest was deliberately in the wrong. I have been able to find excuse for anything but that, not for my own sake but for the sake of the sacred character of him who could say what was not true. Had the truth been told to the Bishop would these scandals have come? I forgive him; I forgive all who had any part in these matters, and so do we all.[47]

She also felt the need to forgive some of her own Sisters. Perhaps what she desired most for her convents was that they should be places of peace, charity and harmony. For this reason she abhorred 'murmuring' and implored her Sisters not to criticise the decisions made by their Superiors. Some of her Sisters failed her notably in these matters and she wrote them a very strong letter stating that she knew of their criticism and insincerity. She went on:

...think that I do not know what they said and how far
they are to blame. But I do know. At the same time I
excuse and with all a mother's heart, I forgive. And as I
freely forgive and wish to forget, so do I entreat you, my
dearly loved ones to forgive from your hearts any Sister
who has pained you, or who you think has wronged you.
I want this letter to bring peace to all your hearts.' [48]

I have, through God's wise permission, at present enemies
at the Terrace. But they are loved enemies and I know
would much rather be friends if they could see and understand the truth.[49]

She loved her enemies

To those who listened to him, Jesus said: 'Love your
enemies'. Few of us take this command to heart. Even
fewer succeed in living it out reasonably well. Those
who do so live it deserve to be called Blessed. Such a
one was Mary MacKillop. Of all those whose writings I
have read, she is the only one who has written: 'I have,
through God's wise permission, at present enemies ...
but they are loved enemies.' This sentence is magnificent.
Only through God's wise permission do others become
our enemies. And in God's wise ordaining we are called
to love even our enemies. Few of us do so. But Mary
MacKillop could write 'they are loved enemies'. Only
deep and serious reflection can tell us how beautifully
and heroically evangelical this attitude really is. For
these words were written, not in times of plenty, but in
the lean years. They were written during the months of
her excommunication by the Bishop of Adelaide.

These were her days of loneliness and her days of
doubt. Loneliness – for Fr Tenison Woods, her Director,
was in Sydney, himself shattered by events and not
answering her letters. Loneliness – for she had difficul-

ties even in finding a place to live: 'I am a Wanderer having no settled place to stay in.' [50] Loneliness – for she could not go near her Sisters lest they be penalised for consorting with her: 'we have been denounced from the pulpit...the poor Sisters...for their connection with the *excommunicated one* who got her due thank God.'[51] They were days of doubt, for she could not understand how priests, whose office she so respected and revered, could be liars. For liars some of them clearly were – she could not deny this even to herself who so longed that such should not be the case. Not only did they tell lies, but the lies they told caused great harm to herself (which she could bear) and to her Sisters – an injustice which she would not stand and barely managed to forgive. Yet forgive she did – and this too, is evidence of heroic virtue.

These were days of suffering, too: 'The pain I have felt about it all has been something terrible, and ...I would have fled where you or anyone else would never find me.'[52]

Mary MacKillop could well be the *saint of reconciliation* for all the world. Our modern world needs to learn what reconciliation means. Forgiving, excusing, is not part of our culture. Suing has become accepted common practice for any mistake made. Someone has to be blamed for anything that goes wrong. Many talk of demanding 'justice' when all they want is revenge. This is far from the true Christian attitude: 'Forgive us as we forgive'. St Augustine points out that it would indeed be bad for us if ours were a God who sued us for all our mistakes: 'It would go ill with the best of us if you were to examine us with your mercy laid aside.'[53]

Mary MacKillop is the saint of reconciliation whom we all need. She excused, and she forgave. Of a priest who had been the main cause of her excommunication and had told lies about her, she wrote: 'I forgive him; I forgive all who had any part in these matters, and so do we all.'[54] To some of her Sisters who had spoken untruths about her, she wrote:

> 'I excuse and with all a mother's heart I forgive. And as I freely forgive and wish to forget, so do I entreat you my dearly loved ones, to forgive from your heart any Sister who has pained you.' [55]

A classic example of Mary Mackillop's virtue of forgiving is spread across the years. Before she founded her religious congregation, she taught school (together with her sister Annie) at Portland. With the two of them earning money, they were able to unite the family together. Mary wrote of this time: 'I have never been so happy'. The happiness was soon to be shattered by the actions of the school's headmaster, a Mr Cusack. The school inspector arrived for a visit to the school. Cusack 'juggled the rolls so that Mary and Annie saw their pupils transferred to his class'. He took credit for their well taught pupils, while they were blamed for the poor showing of his. He went even further and did some cheating by showing answers to the children behind the inspector's back.

Mary's father spoke publicly and strongly about these doings; Annie lost her job, and Mary was blamed for whatever went wrong. 'For four months this storm raged – and I stood alone.' 'God permitted a very bitter enemy to rise up against me, who said such things that all I cared most for turned against me.' This enemy, it seems, was Mr Cusack who was sacked and blamed

Mary for it. There was deep hurt for Mary in all this: she was blamed for another's sin, friends distrusted her, her happy family unity was destroyed, yet later she wrote: 'Some years ago I believed I had an enemy, but I loved him and blamed him not.'[56]

Very succinctly, Mary Cresp writes the final chapter in this story of forgiveness:

> When we read that Mary recognised an old acquaintance at Circular Quay, we are immediately engaged. However, when we discover that this dirty, alcoholic tramp was the schoolmaster whose cheating had led to Mary's disgrace at Portland, the Gospel begins to unfold. For this man Mary sold her watch so that she could get him a suit of clothes and care.[57]

In later and better days, her practical, human charity comes out in the very sensible advice she gives to Superiors of local communities. She obviously has a warm – and very commonsense – regard for her own Sisters:

> Never correct when you are angry and do not suspect too easily – at least do not make your suspicions known too easily. [58]

> And now a word to you all who are in charge of the various communities. Watch most carefully over the health, comfort and happiness of those confided to you. See that poverty be observed – no waste or extravagance, but mind the Sisters have good wholesome food, and plenty of it, and warm clothing, beds etc.... No Sister's health should be allowed to suffer neither should it be endangered by want of proper care on the part of those in charge of her.

> Another matter that I ask each Little Sister to attend to is the study and self-improvement of the members of her community. The part of the day set aside for this should not be interfered with.[59]

Mary could walk the way of Jesus and tell his truth, because she 'lived his life'.

As Fr Clune writes: 'Continuous union with God. My first impression was that she was wrapped up in God. As far as a human being could, she was wrapped up in God.'[60]

1 John Paul II, 20 January 1995.

2 *MacKillop Letterbook*, MacKillop to Woods, 6 March 1869, Mary MacKillop Archives, North Sydney.

3 *Letterbook*, MacKillop to the Sisters, 6 March 1900.

4 MacKillop, *The Necessity for such an Institute of the Sisters of St Joseph to meet the needs of the Australian Church*, August 1873, Mary MacKillop Archives, North Sydney, folio 73, vol 5, no 8.

5 *Letterbook*, MacKillop to the Sisters, 25 March 1873.

6 *Letterbook*, MacKillop to her mother, 6 June 1870.

7 Margaret M Paton, 'Mary MacKillop and the Will of God', *Australiasian Catholic Record*, Vol 74 No 4 (October, 1997), p 456-7.

8 *Letterbook*, MacKillop to Woods, 2 August 1870 and MacKillop to Kirby, 18 July 1874.

9 *Letterbook*, MacKillop to her mother, 21 August 1867.

10 *Ibid*.

11 *Letterbook*, MacKillop to her mother, 21 August 1867.

12 Paton, 'Mary MacKillop...', p 454.

13 *Letterbook*, MacKillop to the Sisters, 14 April 1882 and 4 March 1891.

14 *Letterbook*, MacKillop to the Sisters, 17 December, 1883.

15 *Letterbook*, MacKillop to the Sisters, 14 April 1882.

16 *Letterbook*, MacKillop to the Sisters, 28 February 1890.

17 *Letterbook*, MacKillop to her mother, 21 December 1868.

18 *Letterbook*, MacKillop to the Sisters, 16 December 1900.

19 *Letterbook*, MacKillop to the Sisters, 14 December 1890.

20 Carlo Maria Martini, *Journeying with the Lord: Reflections for every day*,

New York: Alba House, 1987, p 104.

21 *Letterbook*, MacKillop to Woods, 21 October 1871.

22 *Letterbook*, MacKillop to the Sisters, 6 August 1870.

23 *Letterbook*, MacKillop to the Sisters, 14 April 1882.

24 *Letterbook*, MacKillop to Woods, 15 November 1871.

25 *Letterbook*, MacKillop to Woods, 15 November 1871.

26 MacKillop to Kirby, 19/20 May 1873, Irish College Archives, Rome.

27 Letterbook, MacKillop to Woods, November 1869, and MacKillop to the Sisters, 28 February and 18 September 1906.

28 *Letterbook*, MacKillop to Sr Monica, 20 May 1909.

29 *Letterbook*, MacKillop to Sr Annette, 1 December 1898, and MacKillop to the Sisters, 9 March 1890.

30 *Letterbook*, MacKillop to Woods, November 1869, and MacKillop to her brother Donald, 1 October 1884.

31 *Letterbook*, MacKillop to Woods, 19 July 1870.

32 *Letterbook*, MacKillop to Woods, 2 August 1870.

33 *Letterbook*, MacKillop to Woods, 16 August 1870.

34 *Letterbook*, MacKillop to Woods, 8 February 1870.

35 *Letterbook*, MacKillop to Woods, 21 February 1870.

36 *Letterbook*, MacKillop to Woods, 8 February 1870.

37 *Letterbook*, MacKillop to Woods, 21 February 1870.

38 *Letterbook*, MacKillop to Woods, 8 February 1870.

39 *Letterbook*, MacKillop to Woods, 21 February 1870.

40 *Letterbook*, MacKillop to the Adelaide Sisters, 6 August 1870.

41 *Letterbook*, MacKillop to Woods, 4 November 1870.

42 *Letterbook*, MacKillop to Woods, 6 January 1870. 'This is a holy convent (Sisters of Mercy, All Hallows, Brisbane). I'm sure it is. It is poor and the nuns seem full of charity and the love of God.' *Letterbook*, MacKillop to Sr Josephine, May 1880. Testimony of Sr Mechtilde, *Positio Super Causae Introductione*, 7, 10, ad 1.

43 *Letterbook*, MacKillop to the Sisters, 26 April 1873.

44 *Letterbook*, MacKillop to Woods, 3 August 1871.

45 *Letterbook*, MacKillop to her mother, 10 October 1871.

46 *Letterbook*, MacKillop to Woods, 14 October 1871.

47 *Letterbook*, MacKillop to Woods, 30 October 1871.

48 *Letterbook*, MacKillop to the Sisters in South Australia, 14 December 1890.

49 *Letterbook*, MacKillop to her mother, 21 October 1871.

50 *Letterbook*, MacKillop to Woods, 6 October 1871.

51 *Letterbook*, MacKillop to Woods, 14 October 1871.

52 *Letterbook*, MacKillop to Woods, 14 October 1871.

53 St Augustine, *Confessions*.

54 *Letterbook*, MacKillop to Woods, 30 October 1871.

55 *Letterbook*, MacKillop to the Sisters, 14 December 1890.

56 *Letterbook*, MacKillop to Woods, 21 November 1871.

57 M Cresp, 'Reflections on Beatification', 25 January, 1995.

58 *Letterbook*, MacKillop to the Little Sisters (Superiors), 2 March 1890.

59 *Letterbook*, MacKillop to the Little Sisters, 12 March 1899.

60 Testimony of Fr F Clune, *Positio Super Causae Introductione*.

5

Concluding reflections

I shall close this book as I began it – by quoting from the poet Rabindranath Tagore. His writings provide material for Christian reflection, for they are touched by 'a ray of the Truth that enlightens all people.'[1]

Years ago I was introduced to Tagore's work in a meeting of the Pontifical Council, *Cor Unum*, when an Indian lady, invited to lead us in prayer, read us this beautiful story:

> I had gone a-begging from door to door in the village path, when thy golden chariot appeared in the distance like a gorgeous dream and I wondered who was this King of all kings! My hopes were high and methought that my evil days were at an end, and I stood waiting for alms to be given unasked and for wealth scattered on all sides in the dust.
>
> The chariot stopped where I stood. Thy glance fell on me and thou camest down with a smile and I felt that the luck of my life had come at last. Then, of a sudden thou didst hold out thy right hand and say: What hast thou to give to

me? Ah what a kingly jest was it to open thy palm to a
beggar to beg! I was confused and stood undecided, and
then from my wallet I took out the least little grain of corn
and gave it to thee.

But how great was my surprise when, at the day's end I
emptied my bag on the floor to find a least little grain of
gold among the poor heap. I bitterly wept and wished
that I had had the heart to give thee my all.

Eloquent indeed is this story – the story of all of us
who are not saints. When we stand before God we
expect God to give to us. When we cannot avoid giving,
we are inclined to give grudgingly and as little as we
can. It is not easy for us to know that what we cling
to selfishly remains drab and dull. What we give, in
self-forgetfulness, is turned to gold.

And what about this for a way of saying that all
our good is God's gift, sheer grace and divine power at
work within us:

Life of my life, I shall ever try to keep my body pure,
knowing that thy living touch is upon all my limbs.
I shall ever try to keep all untruths out from my thoughts,
knowing that thou art that truth
that has kindled the light of reason in my mind.
I shall ever try to drive all evils away from my heart
and keep my love in flower,
knowing that thou hast thy seat
in the inmost shrine of my heart.
And it shall be my endeavour to reveal thee in all my actions,
knowing it is thy power that gives me the strength to act.

———

Here is thy footstool and there rest thy feet
where live the poorest, the loneliest and the lost.

———

Our master has joyfully taken upon him the bonds of creation;
he is bound with us all forever.

[This is so like St. John's: 'And the Word was made flesh
and dwelt amongst us.' (Jn 1:14)]

My desires are many and my cry is pitiful,
but ever didst thou save me by hard refusals;
and this strong mercy
has been wrought into my life through and through.

Day by day thou art making me worthy
of the simple great gifts that thou gavest to me unasked -
this sky and the light,
this body and the life and the mind.

I have had my invitation to this world's festival,
and thus my life has been blest.

If thou speakest not,
I shall fill my heart with thy silence and endure it.

and finally:

The market day is over
and work is all done for the busy...
I am only waiting for love
to give myself up at last into his hands.

+ E.J. Cuskelly, MSC,
Auxiliary Bishop of Brisbane (retired)
24 January, 1999

---

1 Vatican II, Decree on the Church's Missionary Activity (*Ad gentes*), n 9.

Bishop James Cuskelly

Eugene James Cuskelly, born to Francis and Mary Cuskelly (nee Garske) in Toowoomba, Queensland, on 6 January 1924, was one of five children. He received his school education at the state school in Cooyar, the convent school in Chinchilla and at Downlands College, run by the Missionaries of the Sacred Heart at Toowoomba (1937-1940).

Entering the Missionaries of the Sacred Heart, he undertook theological studies at the Sacred Heart Theological College, Croydon, Victoria, from 1943 to 1947, and at the Pontifical Gregorian University, Rome, from 1947 to 1951. During his studies in Rome he was ordained to the priesthood (on 18 December 1948) and on his return from there his first parish assignment was to Randwick, New South Wales – from 1951 to 1952.

He returned to his alma mater, Sacred Heart Theological College, from 1952 to 1953 as lecturer in dogmatic and spiritual theology, and again from 1956 to 1967, interposing a period as secretary to the Apostolic Delegate from 1954 to 1956. From Croydon he transferred to St Paul's National Seminary, Kensington, New South Wales, in 1967. He remained at Kensington until 1969 when he was appointed Superior General of the Missionaries of the Sacred Heart. This post took him to Rome where he remained until the completion of his term as Superior General in 1981

While in Rome he served from 1976 to 1981 as a member of the Executive Council of the Union of

Superiors General – the consultative council to the Sacred Congregation of Religious – and the Superiors Generals' 'Ecumenical Consultation'. He also represented the Superiors General in the Pontifical Commission *Cor Unum*. In 1977, and again in 1980, he was one of ten Superiors General elected to the Synod of Bishops.

While leading the Missionaries of the Sacred Heart, he made an enormous contribution to the Order's work around the world. At his direction, the Missionaries of the Sacred Heart promoted the cause of Peter To Rot, the Papua New Guinean martyr, who was beatified recently.

He was ordained an auxiliary bishop to Archbishop Rush in Brisbane on 21 July 1982, taking as his motto 'We have learnt to believe in the love God has for us'.

In the following years he served as Chairman of the Australian Bishops' Committee on Doctrine and Morals, was Vicar for Pastoral Planning in the Archdiocese of Brisbane and a member of the Archdiocesan Commission on Ecumenism. As auxiliary bishop, he was widely known for his warmth and easy manner and for his commitment to the policies that flowed from the Second Vatican Council. He retired on 30 April 1996.

Bishop Cuskelly wrote several books, including: *A Heart to Know Thee* (which was translated into German and Spanish), *The Kindness of God*, *No Cowards in the Kingdom*, *Jules Chevalier: Man with a Mission*, *A New Heart and a New Spirit*, and *With a Human Heart*. His writings were influential in the formation of many priests and religious especially throughout the English-speaking world. He died on 21 March 1999, shortly after completing *Walking the Way of Jesus.*